A GENTLEMAN
VOLUNTEER

A GENTLEMAN VOLUNTEER

THE LETTERS OF GEORGE HENNELL
FROM THE PENINSULAR WAR
1812–1813

EDITED BY

MICHAEL GLOVER

HEINEMANN : LONDON

William Heinemann Ltd
10 Upper Grosvenor Street, London W1X 9PA
LONDON   MELBOURNE   TORONTO
JOHANNESBURG   AUCKLAND

First published 1979
Letters © Elizabeth Hennell 1979
Introduction, notes and summaries © Michael Glover 1979

434 29561 2

Printed and bound in Great Britain by
Morrison & Gibb Ltd, London and Edinburgh

CONTENTS

Introduction   1

1 BADAJOZ AND SALAMANCA   7
  April–August 1812
2 SUMMER IN MADRID   34
  August–October 1812
3 RETREAT TO PORTUGAL   56
  November 1812–March 1813
4 'IN FORTUNE'S WAY'   67
  May–June 1813
5 VITORIA   84
  June–July 1813
6 THE PYRENEES   105
  July–August 1813
7 ON THE FRONTIER   119
  August–October 1813
8 THE INVASION OF FRANCE   140
  November–December 1813

Appendices :
  1 Biographical Notes   158
  *2 Officers of the Forty Third Light
     Infantry*   162
  3 Organization of the Light Division   171
Index   173

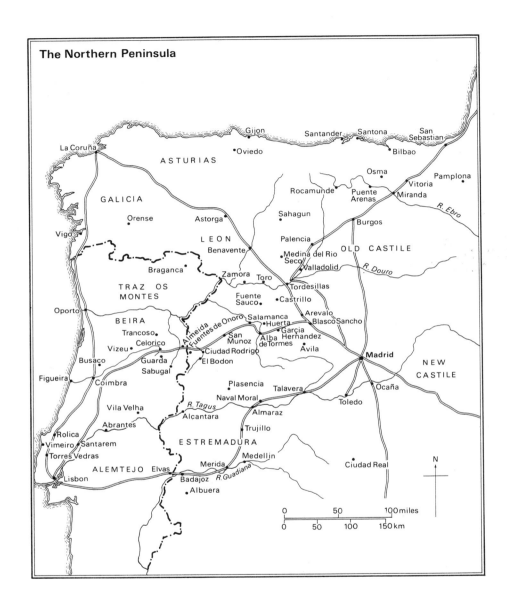

The Northern Peninsula

Gijon

Santander · Santona
San Sebastian

La Coruña

ASTURIAS

· Oviedo
Bilbao

Osma

Pamplona

Rocamunde
Vitoria
Miranda

GALICIA

Puente
Arenas

· Orense
Astorga

Sahagun

R. Ebro

Vigo

Burgos

LEON
Palencia
OLD CASTILE

Benavente
Medina del Rio
Seco

Braganca

TRAZ OS
MONTES

Zamora
Toro

Valladolid
R. Douro

Fuente
Sauco

Tordesillas

Oporto

· Castrillo

BEIRA

Salamanca
Arevalo

Trancoso

Huerta
Blasco Sancho

Almeida
Fuentes de Onoro

San
Munoz

Garcia
Hernandez

Celorico

Vizeu

Alba
de Tormes

Busaco

Guarda

Ciudad Rodrigo

Avila

Madrid

Figueira

Coimbra

Sabugal

El Bodon

NEW
CASTILE

Plasencia

Talavera

Ocaña

Vila Velha

Naval Moral

Toledo

R. Tagus

Almaraz

Abrantes

Alcantara

Rolica

Trujillo

Vimeiro
Santarem

ESTREMADURA

Torres Vedras

Medellin

ALEMTEJO

Elvas

Merida

Ciudad Real

Lisbon

Badajoz
R. Guadiana

· Albuera

N

| 0 | | 50 | | 100 miles |
| 0 | 50 | 100 | 150 km |

INTRODUCTION

The belief persists and is still put about by otherwise reputable historians that the officers of Wellington's army were scions of the aristocracy who obtained their commissions and their promotion by purchase. George Hennell is an example of a far more common type of Napoleonic war officer. He was the son of a Coventry ribbon manufacturer in a moderate way of business whose cousins were silversmiths in the City of London. Two generations back the family was making a modest competence as linen drapers in Kettering. Far from purchasing his commission, George went out to the Peninsula armed only with a letter of introduction to Major General Thomas Picton, the formidable Welsh commander of the Third, the 'Fighting' Division of Wellington's army. He found Picton in the 'Camp before Badajoz' and the general attached him to the Ninety Fourth Foot as a Volunteer. Two days later that regiment took part in the storming of Badajoz and George distinguished himself to such an extent that within six weeks he found himself gazetted as an ensign in the Forty Third Light Infantry, one of the most sought-after regiments in the army.

Volunteers are a very ill-defined category. No mention of them appears in any regulation and there appears to be no other first-hand account by anyone who served in this way. In his *Wellington's Army*, Sir Charles Oman wrote that 'In addition to the officers regularly commissioned, a battalion had often with it one or two "Volunteers" – young men who were practically probationers; they were allowed to come out to an active service battalion on the chance of being gazetted to it without purchase, on their own responsibility. They carried muskets and served in the ranks but were allowed to wear a uniform of a better cloth than that given to the rank and file, and messed with the officers.' It may be noted that Hennell got his commission in a regiment other than the one in which he served as a Volunteer and that the jacket he wore was a normal quartermaster's issue. Since he was not enlisted as a soldier he can have drawn no pay and presumably he had, like all soldiers and, on active service, all officers, to contribute sixpence a day for his rations.

During the Peninsular war 4½ per cent of all new officers gained their first commissions as Volunteers. This was a slightly smaller proportion than those who were promoted from the ranks (5·42 per cent) and rather more than earned their commissions from the Royal Military College (3·9 per cent). The proportion who purchased commissions was slightly less than one in five and in the infantry of the line (where an ensigncy cost £400) only 17 per cent did so. A glance at the last part of Appendix 2 will show that out of twenty-eight ensigns who joined the Forty Third after Hennell, only three purchased. The largest number of new officers in the army either did so from the Militia or were given free commissions on the strength of a recommendation from someone holding the rank of major or above.

Having been born between 1780 and 1785, Hennell was a good deal older than most aspirants to commissions. Three aspirants out of four had not reached their twenty-first birthday when they were commissioned and four out of ten were between fifteen and seventeen. This makes his writing much more mature than that of most young officers and may account for his keen eye for detail as he tried to describe to his brothers and friends a way of life which was quite outside their experience. He not only detailed events as they happened but tried to analyse his own reactions to the dangers and horrors through which he was passing. He illustrated his letters with diagrams and sketches, some of them in great detail since, like the Hennell family to this day, he had a great facility with a pencil. All his opinions are coloured with the strong Unitarian streak which ran through his family and produced a notable religious writer in the next generation. In many of his letters there are deprecatory references to the swearing, drinking and blasphemous habits of his brother officers, to say nothing of the soldiers. It is interesting that this did not prevent him from deliberately getting drunk while on piquet duty in September 1813 (see Letter XXII).

All the twenty-six letters are written with great immediacy, many of them under very uncomfortable circumstances. 'This letter', he wrote in July 1812, 'has been written upon the grass upon a box or anything else I could get.' There is a price for this immediacy. Some of his facts, gathered at second-hand, were wrong. Occasionally he repeats himself and from time to time he creates confusion by using 'he' or 'they' so as to make it hard to understand to whom he is referring. In these cases I have inserted a clarification in square brackets. Otherwise I have left the text (including the occasional obscurity) as it stands with two exceptions:

(i) I have standardized the spelling of the place names, using the maps of Lopez and Faden to which Hennell would have had access.

(ii) I have adjusted the punctuation which, as in so many letters of the period, is partially indicated by dashes of irregular lengths while paragraphs were eschewed in order to save paper.

For the rest I have confined my editing to giving, at the start of each chapter, a short summary of the events in the campaign during the period covered by the letters, and to inserting explanatory foot-notes where needed. In the three appendices are: (i) biographical notes on the more important figures mentioned in the letters; (ii) a list of the officers serving in the Forty Third during the time Hennell spent with it; (iii) an outline organization of the Light Division, the generals and units of which are frequently referred to in the letters.

Two of these letters were written to a family friend, Mr West, the remainder were to his brothers. Although a few are still in their original handwriting, the majority are in contemporary copies made for circulation within the family. Two of them were printed in an abridged form in Sir Richard Levinge's *Historical Records of the Forty Third, Monmouthshire, Light Infantry* (1868) and it is clear that Levinge had access to most if not all of the remaining letters. Twenty-four of them have, however, never previously been published.

Hennell's first regiment, the Ninety Fourth Foot, had some title to regard itself as the oldest regiment in the British army. It was first raised in 1572 but, although its officers and men had been predomi-nately Scottish, it had been in the service of the United Provinces. On the comparatively rare occasions when Holland and Britain were at war the regiment had been permitted to go into suspended animation until the fighting was over. This happy association con-tinued until 1782 when, Holland having espoused the cause of the American colonies, the Dutch government demanded that the officers of their Scots Brigade renounce their allegiance to King George. This they refused to do and sixty-one of them left the Netherlands and were put on the English Half-Pay list. The outbreak of the French Revolutionary war brought them back to full-pay as the Scots Brigade, originally of four battalions but soon shrinking to one which was sent to India in 1797. While there it fought at Seringapatam and, under Sir Arthur Wellesley, at the battle of Argaum. In 1802 it was renamed the Ninety Fourth Foot (Scotch Brigade). Returning to Britain in 1807 it adopted the kilt but lost both that and its Scotch title in 1809 when it was found that there were not enough Scottish recruits to fill the ranks. After a time in the garrison of Cadiz it joined Wellington's army in September 1810 and, before Hennell joined it, had fought at Fuentes de Oñoro and at the storming of Ciudad Rodrigo. After the Napoleonic wars it was disbanded only to be re-established in 1823. After the Cardwell reforms it found itself transformed into the 2nd battalion, Connaught Rangers and, with the rest of the southern Irish regiments, was disbanded in 1922.

The Forty Third (Monmouthshire) Regiment of Foot (Light Infantry), as it was described in the Army List, had first been raised as Fowke's Regiment in 1741. It had fought with Wolfe at Quebec and took part in the American War of Independence from Lexington to Yorktown. It had always been one of the better regiments of the line but it began a sharp ascent to being an outstanding one in 1803 when, with the Fifty Second (Oxfordshire) Foot, it was converted to Light Infantry. The training for its new role was supervised by Sir John Moore and, under his command at Shorncliffe, the two light infantry battalions formed, with the Ninety Fifth (Riflemen), the Light Brigade which was designated as the spearhead of Britain's defence against Napoleon's threatened invasion.

After the Vimeiro and Coruña campaigns the Light Brigade returned to the Peninsula under Brigadier Robert Craufurd, a commander of light troops as great in his different way as Moore himself, and in 1810 it was expanded with Portuguese units to form the Light Division. Craufurd continued to command until he was mortally wounded at Ciudad Rodrigo in January 1812 and the command was eventually given to an officer of the King's German Legion, Charles von Alten, who was, in Wellington's words, 'the best of the Hanoverians'.

The Light Division was the flower of Wellington's army, a fact generally acknowledged by the rest of the force and one cheerfully assumed by those who belonged to it and referred to it simply as *The* Division. We have Wellington's own testimony that they did not flatter themselves since in 1814 he remarked, 'The Light, Third and Fourth Divisions were the *élite* of my army, but the Light had this peculiar perfection. No matter what was the arduous service they were employed on, when I rode up next day, I still found a *division*. They never lost one half of the men other divisions did.'

In 1881 the Forty Third were linked with their old comrades in arms to form the Oxfordshire and Buckinghamshire Light Infantry. More recently the regiment became the 1st battalion, Royal Green Jackets.

April 1812, the time at which George Hennell joined the army, saw the turning-point in the six years of the Peninsular war. Three times, in 1808, 1809 and 1810, the French had invaded Portugal and each time Wellington had driven them out. Twice, once under Moore and once under Wellington, the British had tried to drive deep into Spain and had been forced into hasty retreat. In the summer of 1811 the French armies in Spain had totalled more than 350,000 while Wellington's army could not put into the field more than 60,000 men, of whom a third were Portuguese. Not that Wellington's men were the only enemies the French had to face. Their rapacity had summoned up against them a vast army of *guerrilleros* which, especially in the mountainous districts, ensured that no isolated Frenchman was ever safe, that every A.D.C. riding with a message needed a regiment of cavalry as escort, that every supply convoy had to be protected by a brigade if not a division. At the end of 1811 the situation changed. Napoleon was concentrating all his energies on the coming invasion of Russia. He withdrew 27,000 men from the armies in Spain and restricted the flow of reinforcements that were needed to replace a steady wastage of almost 10,000 men a month and he lost all interest in Spain, leaving the direction of affairs in that country to his brother, King Joseph, and a half a dozen mutually antipathetic army commanders. His last intervention was to order the occupation of Valencia, an irrelevant operation which further dispersed the already overstretched French armies and weakened the force which could oppose Wellington.

Introduction

This was the chance which Wellington was looking for. Before he could invade Spain with safety he had to hold the two fortresses which commanded the roads from Portugal into Spain. One of them, Ciudad Rodrigo, he snatched on 19 January 1812. That left Badajoz, a far stronger fortress than Rodrigo. It stood on the south bank of the Guadiana river, which was nowhere less than three hundred yards wide, and had a curtain wall of twenty-three feet and more, punctuated by thirty-foot bastions. The city was dominated by its castle, standing on a hundred-foot hill overlooking the river. The garrison was more than adequate and the governor, Armand Phillipon, an exceptionally resolute soldier who had already withstood two British attacks in 1811.

On 16 March the allied army crossed the Guadiana on pontoon bridges and invested Badajoz. Nine days later the breaching batteries opened fire on the outworks.

1 Badajoz and Salamanca

The siege guns had been firing on the city for nine days when Hennell joined the Third Division in the 'camp before Badajoz'. On 25 March the outlying fort of the Picurina had been stormed and then the whole of the heavy armament, sixteen 24-pounder guns and smaller weapons, was turned on a length of wall between the Santa Maria and Trinidad bastions at the south-eastern corner of the main wall. Wellington's plan for the assault, first issued on the day Hennell started his first letter, called for three attacks. The main thrust, to be made by the Fourth and Light Divisions, was to be launched at the breaches the guns were battering. To divert attention from this thrust the Fifth Division was to attempt to scale the curtain wall near the river at the north-western corner. Thirdly Picton's division, at the general's own suggestion, was to attempt to escalade the castle, to drag their heavy ladders across the flooded Revillas stream by a narrow mill-dam, scramble up the steep slope of the castle hill and try to get over the wall at what should have been the strongest part of the defences.

Badajoz fell to the assault on the night of 6–7 April and Wellington wrote that its capture 'Affords as strong an instance of the gallantry of our troops as has ever been displayed, but I anxiously hope that I shall never again be the instrument of putting them to such a test as that to which they were put last night.' The storming had cost 3,713 casualties and the survivors indulged themselves in a riot of plunder and drunkenness so intense that it was twenty-four hours before discipline could be restored. A week later the army marched back to the Ciudad Rodrigo front, where they rested for seven weeks while supplies were brought up for their next move. Then, having left a corps under Sir Rowland Hill to watch Badajoz and the French army in Andalusia, Wellington marched eastward on 13 June. He had

48,000 men and his aim was 'to move forward into Castille, and to endeavour to bring Marmont to a general action. . . . I am of opinion that I shall have the advantage in the action, and that this is the period of all others in which such a measure should be tried.'

Marmont's army had a fighting strength of 50,000 but it was widely scattered, one division being as far away as Oviedo in the Asturias. His immediate force was only 15,000 men and, to gain time, he left a garrison of 800 men in three fortified convents at Salamanca. While the allies tackled these the French gathered in their strength and Marmont came forward to see whether he could relieve the garrison. Finding it impossible he retreated to the line of the Douro between Toro and Tordesillas and for the first two weeks of July the two armies faced each other across the broad river. Then, with the whole of his army assembled, Marmont feinted at his right and launched his entire strength across the river at Tordesillas. Wellington was caught on the wrong foot but, after brisk skirmishes at Castrejon and Castillo, he extricated his threatened right wing and the two armies marched parallel to each other, and often within easy cannon shot, southwards towards Salamanca.

On 21 July Wellington's army lay around the south east of the city and the French were approaching them from the east. Knowing, as Marmont did not, that substantial French reinforcements were approaching from other French armies, Wellington was prepared to fall back to Portugal. But Marmont overreached himself; he thought he saw a chance of cutting off the allied rearguard and tried to push his leading divisions round Wellington's right. The movement was ill conducted and the French divisions became strung out. Wellington saw his chance and, muttering 'By God, that will do!' swung up the Third Division on his right to meet, and beat, the leading French troops. Throwing in a heavy cavalry brigade to exploit their success, he launched a solid block of four divisions at the French left centre. By this time Marmont had been incapacitated by a wound and although his successor, Clausel, launched a gallant counter-attack the issue was no longer in doubt. By nightfall the French were streaming away to the east covered by their last intact division. Had a Spanish officer obeyed his orders to hold the bridge at Alba de Tormes the Army of Portugal must have been destroyed. Unfortunately the bridge was left unguarded and the wreck of the French force escaped. They had lost 7,000 killed and wounded, 7,000 more were prisoners and there were so many stragglers that Clausel reported that he had only 20,000 men with the eagles. He led them to Valladolid and beyond, determined above all to get away from the Anglo-Portuguese army, whose casualties had been only 5,000.

LETTER I

MY DEAR FRIEND,

I came here from Lisbon with a detachment by Vila Franca, Santarem, Abrantes, Portalegre and Elvas. We marched 14 days about 18 miles a day, up a hilly country without halting. My feet were at first a little tender but soon got cured. I found the Portuguese behaved very well, if you did so to them, but they have a most forbidding aspect. When you go to them with their billet, my plan was to take notice of them. If an old maid gave the cat a bit of meat, I told its name in English. If a little boy marched across the room, I called him a little soldier: my chocolate was immediately made, my food cooked and in general I met with good accommodations. I must except, however, Abrantes. There the people were the most brutal set I ever saw: had we come among them as thieves they could not have behaved worse. Indeed all the Portuguese seem to think they are not under a grain of obligation to us. They make their market of us and, I believe, many will be sorry when the war is over. Some of the more enlightened think differently. The Portuguese soldiers improve very fast. We have two regiments with us that are very fine ones.[1]

Above I have given you a sketch of Badajoz. We are to storm it tonight. I arrived here the 3rd April at sunset. I delivered my letters of introduction to General Picton that night; he told me to call upon him in the morning. When I did so he attached me to the 94th Regt. and told me my appointment would be according to my exertions.

---

[1] There were, in fact, three Portuguese regiments with the Third Division, the 9th and 21st Line regiments (each of two battalions) and the 12th *Caçadores* (Chasseurs). General Picton, no gentle judge of troops, said of his division a year later: 'There was no difference between the British and the Portuguese, they were equal in their exertions and deserving of an equal portion of the laurel' (letter to Lord Hastings of 26 July 1813).

He sent his aide-de-camp to introduce me to Col. Campbell (the Colonel) as a friend of the general's. I am attached to Capt. McArthur's company.[1] General Picton had promised to promote my advancement all in his power.

The orders are just given to attack in three places, viz: the two breaches, 9 and 10,[2] and to scale the walls near the citadel, nos 3 and 5. Our company are to mount the walls second, so very shortly I shall see real service. It is expected to be sharp work if they do not surrender, which is not likely, General Phillipon being a very determined fellow. The French seem to be short of powder and shot, perhaps they are reserving it for us tonight. They have been firing principally from nos. 5, 3 and 23. They fire a shell or bomb every two minutes. We keep up a constant fire from all our batteries from nos. 13, 14, 15 & 16 on the two breaches, and from nos. 11 & 12 upon the town. I took the sketch from a hill between which and the town there is a plain. There is a ditch about 20 ft. broad before the breach. Of the breach we have a beautiful view. The weather is very fine. I have scarcely seen a cloud since I came to the camp. We go out to look at the breach as you did the comet.

April 9th. I should have sent you the above sooner but have been taken up in seeking for a jackass. The rascally Portuguese stole mine and several others while I was at the storming. I am not sorry for this delay since it will allow me to give you some particulars of the most gallant and interesting affair which they have performed in the Peninsula. I shall give you those facts I witnessed and relate exactly my feelings. The place was to have been attacked on the 5th but, at 6 o'clock parade, orders were given to postpone it for that night.[3]

---

[1] Archibald McArthur was still a lieutenant at this time. He did not get his captaincy until 6 January 1814.

[2] The figures refer to those on Hennell's sketch opposite p. 55.

[3] The Chief Engineer had been wounded in the preliminary operations of the siege on 19 March. He was sufficiently recovered by 5 April to make 'a most attentive examination from various points to obtain the best view he could of the obstacles created by the garrison behind the breaches'. He reported 'that the principal breach appeared to be prepared for an obstinate and protracted resistance'. The storm was therefore postponed for twenty-four hours so that further battering could be done the following day. Orders were also given 'for a continued fire of grape-shot to be kept up on the breaches throughout the night', to prevent the garrison working on their defences. On 6 April a third breach was blown between the Santa Maria and Trinidad bastions.

Alpalhão 16th April. On the 10th we left the camp at Badajoz, on the 12th at Arronches, 13th Portalegre, 14th Alpalhão. The French have been at Castello Branco. Our troops have burned about 3,000 pairs of shoes and a great many barrels of flour to prevent them falling into the hands of the enemy,[1] but I must now give you the particulars of the storming of Badajoz which I promised you before, but first I must tell you of the preparations Phillipon had made to show you what we were going about. He is allowed to be one of the best engineers the French possess, and I assure you he has proved himself so. Altho' our fire was directed to the breach he had fastened a piece of wood into the ground – to this were fixed sword blades, pieces of bayonets, etc. about a foot long, slanting just behind that a chevaux de frise chained at both ends. The centre piece was about a foot square, the points about a yard long from the centre. Behind there was a trench four foot deep and four foot wide; behind that were men eight deep – the first two ranks on the ground who had nothing to do but fire as fast as they could, those behind loading for them. He told them if they stuck to their posts all the men in the world could not enter. Trenches were dug about fifty yards round the breaches in case we should enter – in short, the arrangements for its defence, every body says in judgment, were never surpassed nor the courage displayed by the French ever exceeded.

At 8 o'clock at night on the 6th April our troops were formed without knapsacks. Part of the 5th Division were to scale on the south side of the town. I was in the 3rd Division consisting of about 3,000 men with orders to scale the walls near the citadel. The remainder of the troops principally to attack the grand breach. Half an hour after we were formed we all marched in an indirect way

---

[1] While Wellington was engaged at Badajoz, Marshal Marmont and the French Army of Portugal made a raid into Portugal. This was done on the peremptory orders of Napoleon and against the inclination of Marmont who knew he could achieve nothing without taking Ciudad Rodrigo and Almeida. These he could not attempt since his siege artillery had been captured in January with Rodrigo. In the event he advanced farther south and penetrated as far as Guarda, where he routed some Portuguese militia on 14 April. The depot of stores at Guarda was set on fire to prevent it falling into French hands but when Marmont heard, on 15 April, that Badajoz had fallen and that Wellington was marching towards him he withdrew and the fire was extinguished, many of the stores being saved.

towards the town with strict orders that not a whisper should be heard. I got a soldier's jacket, a firelock & 60 rounds of cartridges and was right hand man of the second company of the 94th Regiment.

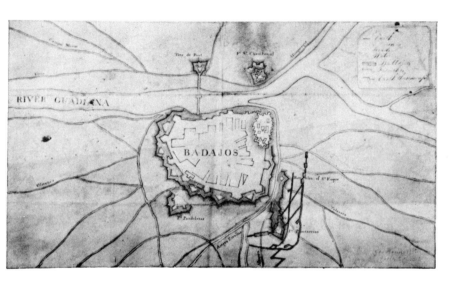

Printed Plan of the Siege of Badajoz, inscribed by George Hennell.

Except the firing of the guns on the breach all was silent on the march till we came within a quarter of a mile of the town. In two minutes it was as if the town was a mine for every yard seemed to send a shot, bombs, cannon balls, grape shot, musquet balls, flying in all directions. On the fire balls alighting, we moved out of the road on to the grass. The cannon balls came hissing by us on the grass and the musquet balls whizzed about our ears. We immediately began to run till we got to about 100 yards of a bridge across the ditch which goes by the breaches close to the wall and runs to the bottom of the hill. There the balls came, as nearly as I can guess, about 20 in a minute within a yard of my head. As we were running one or two dropped on the grass every minute & were left. They now fell very fast. Mr Bogue, nephew of the Revd. Mr B of Gosport, with whom I had dined with Mr [Ensign James] Lang and Mr McArthur, was shot in the knee. When we came to the bridge, about two yards wide and twelve long, the balls came so thick that I had not the least expectation of getting over it alive.[1] After passing the bridge we began to ascend the hill. We were then much crowded as people at a fair. The word was passed for more ladders. We then had to creep on our hands and knees it was so steep and slippery. While creeping Mr Lang received a ball directly in his brain & fell dead. When we got up this rock we came to some palisades within about 20 yards of the walls. The palisades were broken down. Behind them was a ditch 3 ft. deep (no 31). Just behind that a flat place about 6 yards broad. Then a hill 8 ft higher than the ditch & then walls 26 ft high with six or seven ladders against it. The hill is very much like Greenwich hill, about as steep and as high. Just as I passed the palisade ditch there came a shot from a 24 pounder (no. 24) directly above this flat place and twelve men sank together with a groan that would have shook to the soul the nerves of the oldest soldier that ever carried a musket. I believe ten of them never rose again, the nearest was within a foot of me, the farthest not four yards off. It swept like a besom all within its range. The next four steps I took were over this heap. You read of the horrors of war, you little know what it means.

When I got over the hill thrown up with the ditch under the wall the dead and wounded lay so thick we were continually treading upon them (I must tell the facts). The men were not so eager to go up the ladders as I expected they would be. They were as thick as possible in the ditch and, the officers desiring them to go up, I stopped about two minutes likewise. The men were asking 'Where is the 74th?' 'Where is the 94th?' I perceived they were looking for their regiments rather than the ladders. I went up the ladder and when

---

[1] Private Joseph Donaldson of the Ninety Fourth describes this part of the advance as follows: 'being apprized of our intentions, the enemy threw out fire balls in every direction, and from total darkness they changed the approaches into a state light as day; by this means they were enabled to see the direction of our columns, and they opened a fire of round and grape shot which raked through them killing and wounding whole sections. We still advanced, silent as before, save for the groaning of our wounded comrades, until we reached a sort of moat about fifty feet wide formed by the inundation of the river; here we had to pass rank entire, the passage only being capable of admitting one at a time. On this place the enemy had brought their guns to bear, and they kept up such a fire of grape and musketry on it that it was a miracle that any of us escaped.' (*Recollections of the Eventful Life of a Soldier*: Joseph Donaldson (new edn. 1841), p. 156.)

about half way up I called out 'Here is the 94th!' & was glad to see the men begin to mount.[1] In a short time they were all up and formed on a road just over the wall. I believe there were not many of our regiment up before me – at least I was up before the commander of my company (Mr McArthur). I lost him at the heap of slain caused by the grape shot. I forgot to say just before the grape shot came, we were cheering four or five times.

When we got into the citadel, which was directly we got over the wall, no shot, I believe, came among us. The batteries were silenced before we got over & were turned towards the archway from the town to the citadel. We formed opposite the two gateways from the

---

[1] The ladders were 24 feet long. 'They were the common sort of ladder, such as are used by builders; and are made of *castano* (chestnut) trees in the woods nearby by the men of the Staff Corps.' Lieutenant J. E. C. M'Carthy, Fiftieth Foot, who had volunteered as an 'Assistant Engineer', 'received with great satisfaction the charge of erecting scaling ladders', and he described the scene at the foot of the wall : 'The fire was so destructive that it was with difficulty that five ladders were raised on the mound, and I arranged the troops on them successively, according to my instructions. . . . The whole face of the wall, being opposed by the guns of the citadel, was so swept by their discharges of round-shot, broken shells, bundles of cartridges and other missiles, and also from the top of the wall, ignited shells, &c., that it was almost impossible to twinkle an eye on any man before he was knocked down. In such an extremity four of my ladders with troops on them, and an officer on the top of each, were broken successively near the upper ends and slided into the angle of the abutment; dreadful their fall and appalling their appearance at daylight. I was forced to the most excessive perseverance of human exertion and cheered to excite emulation, "Huzza! they are long enough, push them up again!" On the remaining ladder was no officer but a private soldier, in attempting to go over the wall, was shot in the head as soon as he appeared above the parapet and tumbled backwards to the ground when the next man (45th regiment) to him on the ladder instantly sprang over. If he was *not* killed he certainly *deserved a crown of glory in this world* . . . But so numerous were the intrepid that the brave man above-mentioned could only be distinguished as *one* of the bravest of the brave. I instantly cheered "Huzza! there is one over, follow him!" but the circumstance of the ladders being broken delayed the escaladers in this part a short time until the ladders were replaced so as to reach *near* the top of the wall, which enabled the troops to pass over; and I frequently cheered, accompanied by the men, to give notice of the successful perseverance of the escaladers.' (*The Storm of Badajoz* by 'Assistant Engineer' [J. E. C. M'Carthy] (1836), pp. 44–6.)

town with orders to let no force break through us. I was in the front rank of one company.

Phillipon, directly he heard we were in the citadel, ordered 2,000 men to retake it at all events; but, being told the whole of the 3rd Division was there, he said, 'Then give up the town'.[1] One battery kept firing for about two hours after we had got in, but the batteries against the breach were still in half an hour. Part of the 5th Division got into the town on the south side and silenced them. The attack on the breach failed. They attacked a second time and were repulsed, and a third time also, which made Lord Wellington say 'The 3rd Division has saved my honour and gained the town'.[2] There were about fifty prisoners in the citadel. I helped the commander to dress his wound.

When the first fire ball was thrown it was about $\frac{1}{2}$ past 9 o'clock, $\frac{3}{4}$ when we got over the bridge, $\frac{1}{4}$ past 10 when the grape shot came, $\frac{1}{2}$ past 10 when we got into the citadel, and near twelve before all was silent. Phillipon went to Fort Christoval[3] and most of the cavalry got out of the sally port (no. 20)

---

[1] Governor Phillipon sent six companies from his reserve to try to recapture the castle but the gates leading from the castle into the town having been blocked up they could not force an entry. Equally the Third Division could not get into the town without fighting another major action. The event that decided Phillipon to give up the town was the escalade by Fifth Division on the opposite end of the river front. So many troops had been called away to defend the breaches that the Fifth broke in without too much difficulty and the sound of their bugles sounding *Advance* through the streets convinced the garrison that the town could not be held.

[2] This remark seems somewhat uncharacteristic of Wellington but it is quoted in Picton's biography published in 1835 by the Rev. H. B. Robinson who attributed the story to 'a letter from an officer written the day after the storm'. Valuable as was the contribution of both the Third and the Fifth Divisions to the capture of Badajoz, the real heroes were the men of the Fourth and Light Divisions who repeatedly hurled themselves at the obstacles in the breaches that they drew almost the whole of the garrison into their defence. In consequence the safety of the castle had to be entrusted to only three companies, two of them Hessian, about 250 men in all. The Fourth and Light Divisions each lost more than 900 of their British troops, the Third and Fifth 521 and 536 respectively. The Ninety Fourth Regiment was luckier than some units and suffered only 65 casualties.

[3] Fort Christobal was the detached work on the other (north) bank of the Guadiana. It surrendered the following morning.

Soon after daylight, the bugle sounded for two hours plunder.[1] The men were pretty quiet all night, but when the bugle sounded they could not get out of the citadel. They, however, soon broke down the gate and sallied forth. The first door that presented itself was dashed in with the butt end of a musket. I hear our soldiers in some instances behaved very ill – I only saw two [behaving ill] and stopped them both; one was beating an old man, the other ill-using an old woman. One of our officers saw a man go among a number of women and force off all their ear-rings.[2] Those that would not give way [he] broke off a bit of their ear. By the laws of war we are allowed to kill all found in a town that stands a storm[3] and our soldiers declared they would do so, but an Englishman cannot kill in cold blood, for we had not been a $\frac{1}{4}$ of an hour in the citadel before the prisoners passed through as quietly as you might have done.

[15th April] Our regiment did not fire a shot all the time. I saw one instance of bravery which I will relate. Just before the grape shot came, we saw 8 or 9 Frenchmen standing on the edge of a battery (no. 32). One of our regiments all fired at once at them. One or two

---

[1] There is, of course, no bugle call for *Plunder*; presumably the call was *Dismiss*. Donaldson, also of the Ninety Fourth, wrote that 'When the town surrendered and the prisoners were secured, the gate leading into the town from the castle was opened and we were allowed to enter the town for the purpose of plundering it.' (Donaldson *op. cit.*, p. 158.)

[2] Amongst those who had their earrings torn from their ears was Juana Maria de los Dolores de Leon. She was rescued by Captain Smith of the Rifles who married her a few days later, Lord Wellington giving away the bride. Years later, when her husband was Sir Harry Smith and Governor of the Cape of Good Hope, she gave her name to the town of Ladysmith.

[3] The laws of war have always been ill-defined but it was certainly the custom that a garrison which continued to resist after the walls had been breached had no rights. Wellington wrote after the war that 'I believe it has always been understood that the defenders of a fortress stormed have no claim to quarter', and the French worked on the same principle. In fact there was no question of the garrison not being given quarter and the fury of the assailants vented itself on the civilian population, who were allied nationals. It was widely believed that the people of Badajoz were pro-French. There is little evidence for this but the evidence then and now is that the people of Badajoz are a singularly disagreeable crew. The editor was warned of this before he visited the town in the nineteen sixties by Spaniards from other parts of the country and his own experience did nothing to disprove the verdict.

fell, the rest stood like statues. They continued firing for two minutes until they were all killed but two, and they stood about a minute till one of them was shot. I saw the other go down, whether killed or not I do not know.

The town is about the size of Northampton. All the houses near the breach were completely battered down & most of the others much damaged. I got back into camp about 11 o'clock in the morning, washed and dressed myself, got some refreshment and returned to the town. You can have no conception of the scene I witnessed, most of the soldiers drunk, staggering about with their plunder. I retraced my steps of the night before. I passed many wounded, indeed there were some in every place. I saw 8 or 10 shot through the face, their heads one mass of clotted blood, many with limbs shattered, some shot in the body & groaning most piteously and, oh shame to the British soldiers, the fatigued officers could not get the men moved all day from their plunder & intoxication.[1] I found the body of poor Lang, his pantaloons, sword, epaulettes, all taken away. The dead bodies lay in every form, some dashed to pieces by bombs, many naked, and you saw where the balls went – many rolled in the dust & blood & dust sticking all over them. When I came to the spot where the grape shot came, the blood lay very thick but that bore no comparison with the breach. There they lay, one upon the other, two or three deep, many in the ditch half in and half out of the water. In coming out you were obliged to tread on many. I went two or three times to the town, the last time the smell was horrible. You were continually treading upon feet or heads.

---

[1] Quartermaster William Surtees, Ninety Fifth, was with Captain William Percival of his regiment on the morning after the storm and 'hearing the heart-piercing and afflicting groans which arose from the numbers of wounded still lying in the ditch, set to work to get as many of these poor fellows removed as was in our power. This we found a most arduous and difficult undertaking as we could not do it without the aid of a considerable number of men, and it was a work of danger to attempt to force the now lawless soldiery to obey and to stop with us till this work of necessity and humanity was accomplished. All thought of what they owed their wounded comrades was swallowed up in their abominable rage for drink and plunder.' (Surtees : *Twenty Five Years in the Rifle Brigade* (1833), p. 144.) Lieutenant M'Carthy (see note 1, p. 15) had sustained a broken thigh at the foot of the wall. None of his own regiment were present but an officer from another detailed some men to carry him back to camp. As soon as they got out of his sight they put M'Carthy down and went off into the town.

I shall now give you my feelings upon the affair & I doubt not that I shall have your sympathy. I marched into the town in good spirits. When the balls began to whiz I expected every one would strike me. As they increased I minded them less. I viewed calmly the town & to the whizzing of the balls soon became accustomed. When upon the bridge I was thinking where I should be struck. At the bottom of the hill I was accustomed to danger & would have marched up to a cannon's mouth. When the grape shot came I felt much more for those that fell than I did for myself. When I trod upon the heap it was horrible. In the next 20 or 30 steps I trod upon many dead – that was not half so bad. I assure you my reflections were very serious ones and at the moment when I expected instantly to be summoned before the Judge that knows every thought as well as deed. These reflections threw shells into my soul that were more formidable than all the balls that were fired from the French batteries that night. I have the greatest reason for gratitude that at least I was not groaning with a shattered limb but, thank God, not a hair of my head was hurt and I caught no cold. I was never in better health in my life. I have walked through the hospitals, I have seen limbs amputated on the field, the dead lying in heaps like rats after a hunt, some thrown into a ditch. I have seen them afterwards putrid. This horrible scene I have contemplated over & over again.

I dined that day with three officers. One was shot through the knee, one dead. The want of reflection in numbers of the men surprised me. They were singing and swearing and talking of having a damned narrow escape while their comrades lay round them in heaps dead. It was horrible. It was a lesson for me that I did not let pass without taking a walk in the fields to reflect upon. I have an opportunity of doing this.

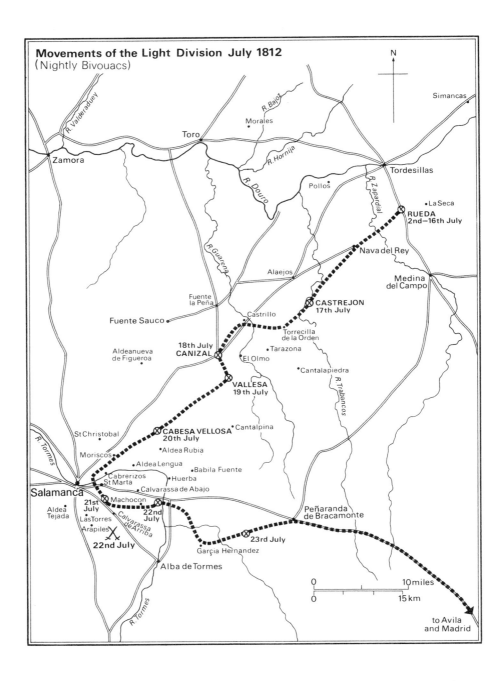

LETTER II

The last I sent was from Niza. . . . We drove the French out of Portugal & then went to Cedavim village, 2½ leagues from the Douro, 5 leagues from Lamego & lay there 5 weeks. There were many kinds of diversions going forward. Major, now Col. Carr of the 83rd Regt invited me to a fishing party for two days. We encamped on a beautiful romantic spot on the banks of the Douro – the jaunt was a very pleasant one, indeed we lived sumptuously for we had roast beef, beef pie, roast mutton, mutton pie, partridges (which we shot), good wine & plenty of good milk in the morning (and is that all, you would say?). In England it would not be much thought of. But it was a Crown and Anchor dinner in Portugal. You have no conception how custom brings all things to their proper place. If we can get tea, biscuits and milk – we live admirably upon our 1 lb of beef a day. I would not have a breakfast on new English bread and fresh butter for a guinea. I have now got into the habits of the country and that would put me out for a month.

There was quite a new kind of diversion set on foot at Cedavim. There was a corps of lancers formed (a burlesque on the Polish lancers); each member was to appear at one time on horseback with a different dress and a lance and he that was most ridiculous was to be commandant. The plunder of Badajoz furnished some excellent materials. One had a large cocked hat flapped down with a beautiful ostrich feather in it, a large gold shawl thrown over his shoulders, a crimson figured satin and quilt over his horse, sky blue satin round his body, his legs dressed with ribbons and large black whiskars [sic], a beautiful flag to his lance & a great many more things. Another had a sheep's skin made into a cap about a yard high like a sugar loaf, a large silk & gold cord twisted round it that hung down to his knees, and a large frill round his neck. Coloured silks round his body, black sheep's skin boots, an enormous pair of spurs, a quizzing glass about the size of a frying pan, and not unlike the rim of one. Another was covered all over with bells and everything you can conceive ridiculous. There were about 40. They paraded on the hill [for] about an hour to the no small diversion of us all and then went to the side of a brook for a pic-nic dinner & I believe as is customary on these occasions, most got drunk. Some went back to their quarters that night, some did not.

A day or two after we had a masquerade at Col. Campbell's. I took my old character of Dicky Gossip & they say I shaved some very well. It went off very well. The Juiz de Fores, Justice of the Peace, and his daughters were very much diverted indeed. On the 4th June[1] we had a grand dinner. The whole brigade dined together in a harbour made of boughs for the occasion. We subscribed 3 dollars each and had a very good dinner & good wine. The colonel gave another masquerade after it. I went as a tipsy cobbler but it was not near so good as the last as there were too many in one character, the half of mine.

We marched next morning at sunrise. Many did not go to bed and have been nearly so ever since. We went by Rodrigo to Salamanca where Marmont was. Arrangements were made to attack them but they retired leaving two regiments in a fort that has been two years fortifying within 200 yards of the town.[2] The whole army except the 6th Division, which had not seen action before in this country, took up a very strong position a league beyond Salamanca. The French came back next day & lay within $1\frac{1}{2}$ miles of us [for] three days. We saw every man of them but they could not see our force as we lay upon a circular hill 4 miles long. A cannonade began at sunset and skirmishing & we were expecting they would come on in the morning, but they durst not, though Marmont did everything he could to relieve the fort, especially as the 6th Division made an unsuccessful attempt to escalade it & had about 70 men killed & wounded.[3] After

---

[1] 4 June was King George the Third's birthday.

[2] Marmont, commanding the French Army of Portugal, had fortified three convents (monasteries) at the southwestern corner of Salamanca where they dominated the only bridge over the Tormes river. When Hennell writes that they were 'within 200 yards of the town' he was only correct because Marmont had demolished much of the university quarter of Salamanca in order to clear the approaches to the convents. They had originally been part of the town.

[3] On 23 June six light companies from the Sixth Division attempted to take the Convent of San Cayetano by escalade. The attack failed with the

they [Marmont and his army] retired, they surrendered the fort and that day Salamanca was crowded with officers.

The Cathedral is a most beautiful building. The structure on the outside & on the inside is immense as is the university. There are several very fine buildings in it. There were many more things to be bought there than at any other place we have been at but all excessively dear. The only thing reasonable was the cream, 6d the tumblerful, cherries 3d & 4d the lb. Spain is far superior to Portugal – a rich soil covered with corn. We passed between Ciudad Rodrigo and Salamanca several valleys of most beautiful grass just ready to cut for hay, five or six miles long & one or two broad, & I understand it would not all be left to rot. You have all heard a great deal about the behaviour of the French to the Spaniards. I believe most of it is true. The French fixed the price of what they did pay for and levied heavy contributions. As we are now the first in advance, & the English have never been here before, they behave much better. The prisoners taken in the fort were excellent soldiers; they were volunteers. They fully expected Marmont would relieve them.

When I returned from Salamanca that night I was hailed with 'I wish you joy. You are gazetted in the 43rd Regt.' 'You are a fortunate fellow indeed. Why, many have been 6, 8 and 12 months volunteers in this country before they got their commissions and you have got it so soon & in the very best regiment in the service.' 'Why, you will have your lieutenancy in that regiment before me, I will lay a wager, who have been here three years.'[1]

I waited upon General Picton next morning to give him my thanks

---

loss of 6 officers and 120 men out of the 300 who made the attempt. Marmont had brought his army close to Salamanca but wisely did not attack Wellington's covering force which was well placed and as strong as the French. On the night of 26–7 June red-hot shot was fired into the roof timbers of San Vincente, the strongest of the convents, setting the building alight. All three surrendered on the 27th and, before dawn on the following day, Marmont started to retreat to the Douro and the rest of his reserves.

[1] Promotion in the Ninety Fourth was sluggish by the standards of regiments serving in the Peninsula. Those who were ensigns at the beginning of 1809 had to wait an average of thirty-seven months to get their lieutenancy by seniority. The 1809 ensigns of the Forty Third got their promotion by seniority in less than fifteen months. The principal reason for this difference lay in the number of death vacancies. The Ninety Fourth had only four officer deaths (two of them in battle) while the Forty Third had twenty (eleven in battle).

for his kind attention to me. He said, 'I am very glad to see you have got your commission.' I said that his so recommending me to so distinguished a regiment would be a great stimulus to my exertions. He said 'It is a very distinguished regiment, I can assure you [and] you will have some fine examples before you but that was all Lord Wellington's doing.' The general seemed to say very cordially, 'I am glad you have got your commission'. Thus has the letter you procured for me got me a commission in the most distinguished regiment in the service and the quickest for promotion, as no one comes from another regiment to this as, if there are any purchases, we have plenty to purchase, so that every alteration gives me a step. By looking at the Army List you will see how I get on.[1] I do again very cordially thank you for your kindness in procuring the letter and hope to do it some time in person.

I saw General Picton again in Salamanca. He had his staff with him. He stopped me & said, 'Well, sir, what are you doing here?' I said, 'I am ordered here to get accoutrements and clothing.' 'Oh, very well,' he smiled and bowed. I bowed & have not seen him since he stopped me at Sabugal, & said 'Well, sir, how do you like soldiering?' I told him very well. All the men & officers say he is an excellent general. They say he is severe & blows up too much but he is a good general. I am sorry to hear he is ill and going home.[2]

When the army marched after Marmont I stayed at Salamanca a

---

[1] The Army List entry for the regiment as it would have been at the time George Hennell was commissioned is set out as Appendix 2, together with the subsequent changes during his service with the Forty Third.

The phrase 'if there is any purchases, we have plenty to purchase' refers to the custom that officers wishing to purchase promotion in their own regiment had, in order of seniority, priority over attempting purchasers from outside. An officer from outside the regiment would only be able to buy in if the first officer for purchase within the regiment was considered unsuitable for promotion (in which case he would quickly be discarded); if no officer wished to purchase; or if, in the opinion of the Commander in Chief, the regiment was in such an unsatisfactory state that promotion should go to an approved officer from outside.

[2] Picton had been wounded in the leg at Badajoz and had also suffered from 'Guadiana fever', a recurrence of the malaria he had contracted at Walcheren in 1809. He was so ill that he remained at Salamanca when the army followed Marmont to the Douro but, on hearing that a battle was likely, he rode up to the army, although he was too ill to stand. He finally set off for England on 17 July.

week to endeavour to get cloth for a jacket, sword, sash, etc. I found a person when I got to Salamanca who made me a good hat, none of the rest could I get there, but I have got them since, except cloth & I have sent to Lisbon for that & wear my blue greatcoat (as many do) with a sash and sabre.

The morning I left Salamanca I was awoke by my window dashing in and stones falling on the roof. The first minute I thought the French had returned but found it to be the ammunition taken out of the fire [fort] set fire to by a Spanish sentinel smoking. It dashed to the ground all the houses within 100 yards circumference and buried the whole of their inhabitants in the ruins and shook the whole city. I was about ¼ mile from it. I went and saw the ruins, saw several dug out, they were in bed when it happened (½ past 6 in the morning). I suppose it killed 40 or 50 men women & children.

I joined [the 43rd] the 10th of July at Rueda, 2 miles from Tordesillas, near Valladolid. We had a dance while there. There were present Lord Worcester, myself, Lord March, several of Lord Wellington's staff & most of the officers of the 43rd. We had a great deal of Spanish dancing which is graceful to them but it appears very indecorous to me & the officers did not make it less so. The lady takes the gentleman round the waist with one arm, and he round her.

While we lay at Rueda the French were at Torrecillas. The first duty I did was the advanced guard of the outlying piquet. I had to send 3 of my men on patrol every hour [for] 24 hours. We left Rueda at dark [16th July]. Next day Marmont came after us, next we marched all night from sun set to sun rise. It was the most fatiguing

---

Hennell's opinion of Picton is confirmed by that of a sergeant of the Forty Fifth who wrote 'General Picton was always very well liked in the division. He was very strict sometimes – in particular about any little bit of plundering that the men would sometimes pick up; and he used always to be talking about how wrong it was to take from the poor people because the countries happened to be at war. He used to have the men flogged but where he flogged many others took life; so our people always thought old Picton a very kind general. Besides this, the men always thought he had their welfare at heart; for every soldier in the division knew that if he had anything to complain of, old Picton would listen to him and, if he could, set him right.' (H. C. Wylly, *History of the Sherwood Foresters* (1929), i 216.) Private Donaldson wrote, 'No man could blame with more severity when occasion required [but] he was no niggard of his praise when it was deserved. Nothing could surpass his calm intrepidity and bravery in danger: and his presence in battle had the effect of a talisman.' (Donaldson *op. cit.*, p. 99.)

march, the soldiers say, they ever had in this country. I walked &
carried the Colours. I was very tired indeed.

The next morning [18th July] the first thing I saw was skirmishing
within ½ a mile of us. We marched & took up our position on the side
of a large hill. Our cavalry & guns were engaged for about 2 hours.
The cannon balls came over us and shells burst near us but none
hurt.[1] I saw come walking towards us, led by 2 soldiers, a cavalry
officer. When he came to us he was perfectly sensible and had walked
about ½ a mile. He asked the surgeon if he should make up his mind
[that he was dying]. The surgeon told him he must not let his spirits
droop. A cannon ball had taken his right breast off & his arm was
smashed to a mummy close to the shoulder. He died 3 hours after.[2]
5 minutes after a private of dragoons was brought in a blanket with
his leg shot completely off at the knee, & the leg & foot lying by his
side. When I came up to the officer I looked into his body & saw
his lungs.

This letter has been written upon the grass upon a box or anything
I could get.

YOURS &c.
G.H.

---

[1] This was the action at Castrejon when the Fourth and Light Divisions
and a cavalry brigade found themselves unexpectedly assailed by most of
Marmont's army, which had slipped over the Douro at Tordesillas. Wellington came up to their support with two more cavalry brigades and the
divisions were extricated with little loss though not before Wellington had
been so near to being overrun by French cavalry that he had to draw his
sword to defend himself.

[2] William Napier, who was commanding the Forty Third at this time,
wrote : 'Suddenly a dismounted cavalry officer stalked from the midst of the
smoke towards the line of infantry with a gait particularly rigid, and he
appeared to hold a bloody handkerchief to his heart; but that which seemed
a cloth was a broad and dreadful wound. A bullet had entirely effaced the
flesh from his left shoulder and from his breast, and had carried away part
of his ribs, his heart was bared and its movement plainly discerned. It was
a piteous and yet noble sight, for his countenance though ghastly was firm,
his step scarcely indicated weakness, and his voice never faltered : this un-
yielding man's name was Williams [Cornet William Williams, Eleventh
Light Dragoons]. He died a short distance from the field of battle, and it was
said in the arms of his son, a youth of fourteen who had followed his father
to the Peninsula in the hopes of obtaining a commission, for they were not
affluent.' (Napier, *History*, iv 254.)

George Hennell, from a miniature portrait in the
possession of Mr Percy Hennell

Lt-Gen. Sir Thomas Picton, painted by M. A. Shee
(*National Portrait Gallery*)

LETTER III

I had no conception that my letters would be so much read. I assure you the 2½ dollars[1] I left Salamanca with a month ago are all I have had to live upon except my rations & I have had dysentery this week past. I am better now. Money will come to the regiment today. If I had £20 in hand I think I could send you a bill, payable in London, for £40 in the course of a month or two. The other day I could have bought a horse for 12 dollars that I could have sold in a week after for 60, if I had the dollars in my pocket & these things often occur in this country especially when the enemy are retiring and, for a good bill on England you may sell anything & for your own price almost.

I find that my description of Badajoz gave a great deal of pleasure to many & it gave me great pleasure to find that many approved the style of writing. David sent me Mrs West's note. On reading it, to have the good wishes of wise & good people is exceedingly gratifying, but to have their good opinion is sterling worth. I shall now make a point of writing constantly when I have the opportunity & send when I have a sheet full. I think you may expect one at least every month. You had better read the letter to West [Letter II] before you go any further, as this begins where his leaves off. They both go by the same packet. I have just received of the Paymaster 25 dollars on account.

I think it was on the 17th July that the skirmishing began. We

---

[1] The peacetime rate for the Spanish dollar was four shillings but it strengthened steadily against the pound throughout the war since it could be backed against South American gold while Britain was constantly short of gold, due to her policy of subsidizing her allies in specie. In March 1812 it was worth 5s 8d and by February 1814 'dollars cannot be had under 7/0d.' Anyone attempting to change sterling into dollars was likely to find his pounds discounted by up to 25% on the transaction.

marched the night before from sun rise to sun set without halting 10 minutes. We marched thro' a village upon a hill where the cavalry officer came by wounded. Then I saw the first charge I ever saw. About 100 of the enemy's cavalry charged about the same number of ours on an opposite hill about a ¼ of a mile from us. Ours formed in a line but when they (the enemy) came up, to our disgrace, ours retired. All our officers were in a perfect rage. We ought to have had the whole of them.[1] The French moved on in a westerly direction & we moved too and took the lead of our army.

About 11 o'clock in the morning [18 Jul 12] we moved in open column within a ¼ of a mile of the French and neither of us fired a shot though moving in the same direction in a plain. They took up a strong position on their right. We moved on & took up ours beyond. That evening the French moved up a hill in close column & deployed. It was the next hill to the one we were upon, about ½ a mile off. The 4th Division allowed them to come to the top before they fired a shot. They gave them a volley & charged them down the hill, killing them as fast as they could with their bayonets & their officers were obliged to assist with their swords, but in retiring they opened a destructive cannonade which killed about a quarter of the number we killed of theirs.[2]

---

[1] In the account by John Cooke, also a subaltern in the Forty Third, of this incident in the action at Castrejon the French actually charged home among the British light dragoons and 'overthrew' them. What actually occurred is described in his diary by Captain William Tomkinson, Sixteenth Light Dragoons, who was present with the cavalry brigade : 'On the left two squadrons, one of the 11th and the 12th [Light Dragoons], were supporting two guns of Major Ross's troop. The squadrons were supporting one another and, on the advance of some of the enemy's cavalry (inferior to the two squadrons), the one in front went about. Some of Marshal Beresford's staff seeing this, conceived the guns were in danger, rode up to the retiring squadron calling "Threes about!" This of course put the other squadron about in the place of fronting the one already retiring. One person gave one word, one another, and the enemy's cavalry came up to the guns. There was no harm done, and our dragoons (the 11th) immediately advanced and drove them back.' (W. Tomkinson, *Diary of a Cavalry Officer* (1894), p. 181.)

[2] At Castrillo, Clausel, who commanded one column of Marmont's army, tried to cut off the left of Wellington's army. Unsupported by the marshal he was severely handled, losing about 700 men (including 6 officers and 240 men taken prisoner). The allied army lost 525 men that day but the

Next day we all lay still till about 11 o'clock in the afternoon [*sic*]. The French began to move along a ridge of hills towards Salamanca. We moved parallel to them & about 7 o'clock the Light Division formed line directly opposite to them, a deep valley between. I had the colours. Our cannon opened before we formed line. We had not formed 2 minutes before a very warm cannonade opened upon us. A ball came just over my head about a foot. A cannon ball makes a tremendous whizz as it passes you. The old soldiers always burst out a-laughing when they see the young ones dip down their heads, which they generally do when a ball passes within a foot or two of them. [We] were ordered to sit down & in a few minutes rose and retired to a line, about 500 yards, & formed a square. All the other divisions came up that night. We slept that night as we always do when near the enemy, the men to be ready in a moment. About two o'clock in the morning somebody fired a shot which frightened the horses & awoke us all, tumbling over each other. We all thought the French upon us, but order was soon restored & we fell in. The whole, both French & us, moved directly towards Salamanca. We halted 3 or four leagues off.

That night we crossed the river [Tormes] in direct line for Ciudad Rodrigo, the French pushing forward, endeavouring to turn our right. We had a tremendous storm of thunder & lightning with heavy rain. Next morning we moved about 2 miles & halted upon a hill. The 1st, 4th, 5th & 6th Divisions before us on a hill opposite the enemy. The 3rd Division passed through Salamanca & lay on the right. There was cannonading all day.

About 4 o'clock in the afternoon the French pushed forward to turn our right. The action began. We had from the hill a beautiful view of the whole. We saw our columns move forward tho' the enemy kept up a heavy cannonade. At the same time the 3rd Division moved forward to a hill occupied by the enemy. We saw distinctly every shell burst. When they came near a very heavy fire opened. We saw them charge & drive the French from the hill. We were ordered to march about 7 o'clock & came up with the enemy about sun set. We never load until we come close up. When we came under the hill the enemy were upon, Ld. Wellington passed us & said, 'Come fix your bayonets, my brave fellows.' We did, and sent out skirmishers &

figure includes about 50 stragglers left behind during the hard marching under a hot sun.

advanced in a line that delighted Lord Wellington. I hear he talked of nothing else next morning at breakfast.[1]

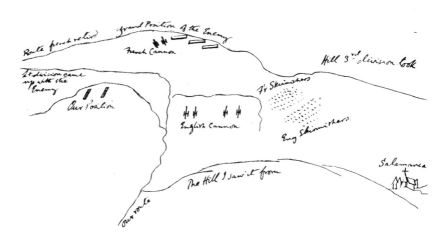

Hennell's sketchmap of the Battle of Salamanca, 22 July 1812.

10th August, 2 leags S.W. of Segovia.

By this time it was quite dark [and] our skirmishers (3rd Caça-

---

[1] The Light Division, for once, played little part in the battle of Salamanca, being on the extreme left of Wellington's order of battle while the fighting was mainly on the right and centre. The whole division suffered only 44 casualties. The Forty Third had two officers (Captain Haverfield and Lieutenant Ridout) and fifteen men wounded.

It was not until the badly mauled French were retreating that the Light was called upon to head the pursuit. Wellington rode with the commanding officer of the Forty Third, William Napier, who described how 'after dusk the Duke rode up *alone* behind my regiment, and I joined him; he was giving me some orders when a ball passed through his left holster and struck his thigh; he put his hand to the place and his countenance changed for an instant, but only for an instant; and to my eager inquiry if he was hurt, he replied, sharply, "No!" and went on with his orders.' (*Life of Gen. Sir William Napier*, Ed: H. A. Bruce (1864), p. 101.)

dores) opened upon them upon the brow of a hill and the French immediately returned it which passed mostly over our heads. We had express orders not to fire until ordered. Our regiment was well prepared to give them an excellent charge but they had received another lesson that afternoon that they will not forget in a twelve-month. Had they stayed still till we came up twenty yards further they might have given us a most destructive volley but they rapidly fired a volley or two that passed mostly over our heads and they ran away. Both the sergeants of my company were slightly wounded.

We advanced in line $\frac{1}{2}$ a mile over corn and ploughed lands. Then [we] formed sections of a company, keeping our distance & marched 2 or 3 miles over bushes and ploughed lands. On passing a wood our skirmishers, who were always about 300 yards in advance, opened a fire. We were in a good line in 5 minutes (it was only a few cavalry in a wood) & advanced dressing by the Colours over horrid roads with numerous pebbles another league. We halted and slept about 10 o'clock till sun rise, then we advanced & crossed the river $1\frac{1}{2}$ leagues above Salamanca & about 11 o'clock we came to a plain surrounded by hills where the German Hussars came up with the enemy. They (the enemy) formed a square but soon retired in the greatest disorder, throwing away everything that impeded their running.[1] We took a great many prisoners. It was about two hours before we came up. You have frequently seen paintings of a field of battle with a hussar & his horse lying just as they fell & weltering in their gore : another with his head cleft in two : many in all positions, some dead, some wounded. This was one of those scenes for a mile. Every step was over cartridge boxes, belts, arms & ammunition of every kind and their cooking utensils, but when we came to the hill their arms lay in columns and bodies very thick. They had made a slight stand there and our Germans rode into the midst of them.

---

[1] The action at Garçia Hernandez on 23 July 1812 was the greatest triumph of Wellington's cavalry during the war. The two regiments of Dragoons of the King's German Legion, 'huge men on huge horses', charged and broke two formed squares of French infantry, a feat almost unrivalled against good troops. Only 770 men charged and they suffered 127 casualties but they inflicted a loss of 1,100 men on the French.

Curiously John Cooke also attributes this exploit to the Hussars rather than the Dragoons of the Legion.

There was a great number killed upon the spot but they put them entirely to rout. Everybody said how well the Germans fought. Mr Cobbe would have said so had he been present. We just got on to the top of the hill to see them going up the next & upon this to see them going up the next. We then halted for the night.

We saw no more of Marmont's army nor shall we, I think, for some time. They are gone in a shocking state to Burgos. They left at Valladolid 1,800 sick.[1] When we were about 7 miles off the banks of the Douro I was out with my company on an outlying piquet about $\frac{1}{2}$ a mile from the town. They say Marmont was buried.[2] I smelled a horrid smell & when I had laid down the sergeant came and told me that a French general had been buried there & that the Spaniards had dug him up for his clothes. It was general Fevy or some such name.[3] He laid about 3 yds off but I had got to the windward of him so did not move and slept very soundly by his side. I was ill of the dysentery or should have gone to Valladolid.

We next day moved in the direction for Segovia and have marched every day since. We are now within 12 leagues of Madrid & most of us expect to see it soon. There is a mail now making up for England. I shall begin my next letter perhaps tomorrow, you may expect it [on the] next or next but one packet. Of course you will show Mr West this. I have been obliged to purchase another horse not because I was the only officer in the Light Division who did not ride but [because] I could not possibly get on without it. The time we marched all night completely knocked me up. I have bought a very fine pony for 35 dollars to be paid in September. So there goes my

---

[1] Only 800 sick and wounded who could not be transported were left at Valladolid although a further 300 prisoners were taken near the city by a guerrilla band. Seventeen guns were also found in Valladolid and a large magazine of stores.

[2] Although the rumour was rife in the British army that Marmont had been killed, he was in fact only seriously wounded with a broken right arm and two wounds in his side. He lived until 1852.

[3] This was General Claude François Ferey (1771–1812), an old adversary of the Light Division. William Napier wrote to his wife on 3 August, 'tell George [his brother in the Fifty Second] that poor General Ferey died of his wounds at Olmedo; and the fine-spirited Spaniards dug up his body and bruised his head with stones. For the honour of the Light Division I have buried him again in spite of them.' (Napier, *op. cit.*, 109.)

bât & forage money[1] but it is well worth it. The comfort of riding is great indeed. With the dysentery I have had this fortnight I could not have marched a mile. I am much better since I have got money. I have got rice, eggs, pigeons, &c, so that my 25 dollars will not last more than a month. I intended it should be two. I wrote you from Lisbon when I was there and waited till my commission came as I should have been much mortified to have sent you word I was recommended to the 43rd if I had not got into it.

Y*our* &c.
G.H.

---

[1] All officers on foreign service were paid sixpence a day for the forage rations of bât animals to carry their baggage in the field. A lieutenant colonel commanding a battalion was allowed ten rations, a captain with his company had five. Subaltern officers were granted only one ration. When a battalion was sent on foreign service each officer was given an advance of 200 days bât and forage money and a further grant (£7.10s for lieutenant colonels, £3.15s for subalterns) known as baggage money. The *Regulations for the Issue of Bât and Forage* (May 1809) do not cover the event of an officer like Hennell who was commissioned in the field but it must be assumed that he received his advance and grant, the princely sum of £8.15s, as soon after his name appeared in the Gazette, if the Paymaster had sufficient funds to pay him. It was not unusual for the officers of the army to have their pay six months in arrears due to lack of coin in the military chest. No outfit allowance was payable, though an ensign's uniform could scarcely cost less than £50 and he would have to pay £4.11s.10d to have his commission registered at the War Office. When he became a lieutenant his fee to the War Office would be £6.11s.10d.

2 Summer in Madrid

The completeness of the victory at Salamanca set Wellington a problem which was all but insoluble. The French Army of Portugal, now under Clausel, was out of the game for the time being and to pursue it too far would do the Anglo-Portuguese army, now at the limit of its supply line, more damage than it could inflict. Having driven it over the Douro and occupied Valladolid (30 July), Wellington called a halt. He could not ignore the dangers represented by the other French armies in Spain while his own force, including the corps he had left around Badajoz, amounted to only 30,000 British effectives and less than 25,000 Portuguese. Some help could be expected from Spanish regular armies but it was hard to guess how much would be forthcoming and how effective it would be.

Against this the French had 35,000 men in the north on whom Clausel was rallying his 30,000 survivors from Salamanca. On the allied right were King Joseph's 15,000 men around Madrid and behind them more than 65,000 Frenchmen on the eastern side of Spain from the French frontier to Valencia. Finally Soult had 60,000 effectives in Andalusia. Even without reinforcements from France it would not be difficult for King Joseph to concentrate 100,000 men against the Anglo-Portuguese army and such a force must drive them back to Portugal – if they could get there.

Wellington therefore decided to take up a central position and deal with French counter-measures as they occurred. His first step was to occupy Madrid. The capital was not a significant military objective but its political importance was considerable as a rallying point to the Spanish people, as an encouragement to the British and as a signal to oppressed Europe that Napoleon's troops were not invincible. It also gave him the possibility of resting his southern flank on the Tagus, which by autumn would probably (but actually did not) become unfordable. He entered Madrid in triumph on 12 August while King Joseph trailed disconsolately southward to meet Marshal Suchet in Valencia at the end of the month. Meanwhile Soult, with the worst possible grace, had abandoned the siege of Cadiz on 24 August and also set off to join Suchet in Valencia.

In the hope of being able to bottle the northern French armies up in the valley of the Ebro, Wellington set off at the beginning of September to capture Burgos, leaving his three best, and most tired, divisions near Madrid where they were joined by the corps from Badajoz under Hill who, since Soult left the south, had no enemy opposing them.

Burgos was Wellington's least successful operation, partly because he underestimated its strength, saying, 'It was not unlike a hill fort in India and I had got into a great many of them.' Moreover he was not prepared to risk his heavy artillery for the siege. Twenty-four-pounder battering guns travelled with agonizing slowness – on good roads each one needed five pairs of oxen to cover six miles a day in fine weather – and Wellington was far from sure that he would have time to get them forward or, if the French attacked in force, to bring them back. He therefore relied on three 18-pounders which were far from adequate for their task. On top of that the French garrison of the castle of Burgos fought with remarkable staunchness and the allied troops who made the attacks were not the equal of those who had stormed Ciudad Rodrigo and Badajoz and were resting at Madrid.

By mid-October 2,000 casualties had been incurred at Burgos, the castle was still unsubdued and Wellington admitted that he was in 'the worst military situation I was ever in'. Fifty-three thousand French troops were advancing on Burgos where he could oppose them with only 35,000, of whom a third were Spaniards. On the Tagus Sir Rowland Hill had 43,000 men (of whom 12,000 were Spaniards) and, from the south, King Joseph and Soult were advancing with 61,000. Wellington ordered both parts of the army to withdraw to the area of Salamanca. At almost the same moment Napoleon was beginning to retreat from Moscow.

LETTER IV

I had the honour of bringing the colours of the 43rd into this city this morning : our brigade is now quartered in the town. We have been within a league of it these five days. About 21 miles from here is a chain of mountains that runs all through Portugal & most part of Spain. We crossed them & halted one day in a park about 1 league from the Escorial, a kind of monastery or palace where the kings of Spain were fond of being at. It is delightfully situated on a hill close under a chain of mountains with a most extensive prospect far beyond Madrid. The chapel is the principal part of the building and it is a most beautiful one.[1] There is a fine painting of some saint who was roasted upon a gridiron and the whole building is in the shape of one. The rooms of the palace are all stripped of their hangings, whether by the French or to prevent the guerrillas taking them I do not know. I think the latter.

The most complete thing I ever saw in my life is the sepulchre where all the kings are buried. You go down about 40 steps by a winding archway about 2 yards broad & 2 high, circular at top, empanelled beautifully, 5 or 6 lamps hanging from the centre about 4 yards from each other. The vault is an octagon. The entrance takes up one partition and a gold crucifix opposite another. The other six are divided into four recesses each of which contains an urn, all full except four. The ceiling is empanelled likewise & beautifully arched, the octagon meeting in a point from whence the lamp is suspended. With the exceptions of the lamps, crucifix, brass plate & feet of the

---

[1] The palace of El Escorial, thirty miles from Madrid, was dedicated to St Lawrence, a native of Huesca, who was slow-roasted on a gridiron for his Christian beliefs in A.D. 261. It was built by Philip II between 1559 and 1584 and combined a royal mausoleum, monastery and royal palace, the whole being in the shape of a gridiron.

urns, the whole steps, sides &c. everything is of marble, the most beautiful variety of it you can conceive, inlaid with the greatest taste, all very finely polished. When the lamps are lighted it must be far the most beautiful place I ever saw. The air is free from any offensive smell as the bodies are embalmed. You leave a hot climate to go down into a cool place free from damp. Still, to go down there & contemplate death must be a refined pleasure which none but those who can think upon death with pleasure can have any conception of.[1] King Joseph was at the Escorial a few days before me. I should have been glad to have met him there but he left a day or two before I got there, so that we have not had the pleasure of meeting yet.

The next day we came 4 leagues & next to that a village a league from here. King Joseph with his army retired as we came in, leaving a fort well fortified and an immense quantity of stores & cannon with 1,800 very fine French soldiers. They surrendered without firing a gun just as the 3rd & 7th Divisions were going to storm it.[2] The 7th Division came into the city first and then the 3rd.

---

[1] This was the *Pantéon de los Reyes* where the kings of Spain and their mothers were buried from Charles V onward (except Philip IV and Ferdinand VI). It is described in Richard Ford's guide book to Spain of 1845. 'Descending by a green and yellow coloured jasper lined staircase, at the bottom is the *Pantéon*, an octagon of 36 ft. in diameter by 38 ft. high. The materials are dark polished marbles and gilt bronze; the angels are by Ceroni of Milan; the tawdry chandelier is by Virgilio Franchi of Genoa; the crucifix is by Pedro Tacca. There are 26 niches hollowed in the 8 sides, with black marble sarcophagi, which are too classical to create a Christian sentiment; the names of the deceased are written on each; those which are filled are inscribed with the name of the occupant; the empty ones await future kings . . . None are buried here save kings and the mothers of kings, for etiquette and precedence in Spain survive the grave; and to preserve propriety the males are placed separately and opposite to the females.'

[2] When King Joseph left Madrid he put a garrison into a fort, built to overawe the civilian population, in the Retiro park. It might have taken some trouble to subdue but when the Third and Seventh Divisions bloodlessly took the outermost perimeter wall on the night of 13–14 August the governor found himself dependent on one small well and surrendered with 1,800 men. Wellington reported, 'We have found in the place 189 pieces of brass ordnance in excellent condition, 900 barrels of powder, 20,000 stand of arms [i.e. muskets complete with bayonets and accoutrements] and considerable magazines of clothing, provisions and ammunition. We have likewise found the eagles of the 12th and 51st regiments, which I forward to England.' (WD ix 359.) The two eagles are now at Chelsea Hospital.

The inhabitants are ready to pull the officers off their horses with joy and they show Lord Wellington much more respect than King Joseph.[1] Madrid has suffered very much indeed by the French and they gave us a very cordial reception. After the French have been 4 or 5 years here telling them of the great things Buonaparte has done and will do and to their very great pleasure seeing them driven from their capital without firing a gun and King Joseph's palace made headquarters for the British army, has given them a very high opinion of a British officer & we perceive it as we walk the street. The lady at the window, immediately she sees you, touches the one next to her to look and they are all ready the moment you make a slight inclination of the head & smile, to return it more cordially with a 'God bless you, English'. This we have from all classes. The people are much more enlightened here than any I have ever seen. You meet with much more politeness & not so much of that sordid spirit there is about Salamanca.

I was ill of a dysentery or should have gone to Valladolid & Segovia as we passed within a league of each. I got well two days ago & I have been enjoying myself since as there are the most beautiful grapes and melons to be had for very little. I take them with caution. The squares are covered with fruit stalls as the inhabitants live mostly on fruit and vegetables. Bread is much better here than any I have had since I left England. There are eating houses where may be had fried fish in oil, vegetables &c. They have oil to almost everything. At others, mutton, beef, partridges, rabbits &c., about as dear as in England but the houses are so very filthy you cannot go in them, and there are taverns much the same as in England only worse, & every dish dressed in French fashion but they are too expensive for a subaltern's pay. I dined once at the best and cheapest of them and shall not again (except invited) & I had about 7 or 8 dishes brought me with about 3 mouthfulls on each – half a pigeon, another, a piece of sausage, another, a bit of cold mutton, 1 [of] soup, 1 dish of vegetables which I desired him to remove & give me potatoes, a bottle [of] thin port wine, melons and grapes after dinner. It cost me 6/-; the wine was not one.

---

[1] Wellington wrote to a friend on 17 August, 'I am among a people mad with joy with their deliverance from their oppressors. God send that my good fortune may continue, and that I may be the instrument of securing their independence and happiness.' (SD vii 384.)

20th August. I have seen the palace and museum.[1] The palace is adjoining the city – a square building in the centre [? of a park]. There is a balcony all round with blinds of canvas which makes it very cool. The rooms are most elegantly fitted up and the ceilings painted far better than any I have seen & those are Stowe, Boughton, Burleigh &c. There is, I believe the original painting of Buonaparte crossing the Alps. The face is beautifully painted & they say it is one of the best likenesses of him that has been taken. It is so natural you may almost suppose yourself receiving the commands he is giving. The dining room has beautiful bronze statues larger than life & is hung with the richest crimson velvet I ever saw, & gold fringes. There are in several rooms some fine pieces (French ones) exceedingly elegant, white ivory & gold figures, burnished & dead gold intermixed. I expect I have not seen all the palace. The outside is about as handsome as Stowe House but has not the advantage of gardens round it. The square in front is about as large as Bloomsbury Square. I shall see it again & if anything more occurs shall send it in my next.

The museum is about the size of the British [Museum] but not near so valuable though there are very pleasing things in it [such] as a specimen of the different kinds of marble found in the different provinces of Spain. Among fossils there is a piece of Derbyshire stone, written upon from Northumberland. There are all kinds of wild beasts stuffed & fixed in their proper attitudes. There is a most excellent one on the old fable of a monkey taking the cat's paw to take the roast chestnuts from the fire. Puss in a high rage, scolding with all her teeth visible, but the monkey has her so completely fixed, his two hind legs holding her, his right fore-leg guiding her paw with the chestnut & his left securing her right. He seems to be very anxious for the chestnut & there is a smiling grin, very expressive of the full enjoyment of the joke, and sufficient caution to ensure its success.

---

[1] The Palacio Real was built 1738–64 by Filippo Juvara and Battista Sacchetti. When Napoleon saw it he remarked to his brother, King Joseph, '*Vous serez mieux logé que moi.*'

The museum Hennell describes was probably the *Real Academia de Bellas Artes* (*Academia de Nobles Artes de San Fernando*) which in those days had attached to it a collection of natural history, instituted by Charles III, which included a remarkable collection of marbles. It was pillaged by the French when they finally left Madrid in 1813.

There is another of a monkey caught in a trap and a fox passing by the monkey [which] has a very different countenance from the last – a most pitiful face imploring the fox to assist him, and Reynard is considering how he shall act. There are all kinds of fish, preserved in their form & colour, likewise birds, insects, &c.

I think I shall go to the play, partly to give you a description & partly to see it myself. I have no doubt once will satisfy us.

I shall begin another [letter] directly & if it gives you any pleasure, I assure you all it does

YOURS &c.
GH.

LETTER V

Madrid, 25th August 1812.

DEAR BROTHERS,

I wish I could place the melon I have just sent off my table upon yours. It is much larger than any I have seen in England and cost 7d. There is very little meat in this country. The middling & lower orders scarcely ever taste it & the higher classes very seldom. The markets here supply the following things – mutton, 1/- the pound; hares, 3/- or 4/- each; partridges, 2/- each; pigeons, 6d; bread, 1/- the pound; vegetables & fruit. The shops have no glass windows. The streets are pitched and paved & about as broad as those of London, the houses in general better, many of them very tastily painted both in & outside. The carriages like the heaviest & worst of our hackney coaches. There are a great number of idle Spanish fops about every part of the town. I do not know what ideas you may have formed of a dashing Spaniard. For myself, I expected to see a fine fellow with a neat curious hat, a cloak of velvet with sleeves slit with satin between of another colour, breeches the same, a handsome satin waistcoat, neat buckles & a small pair of shoes. Imagine then a tall thin figure, thin lank jaws that seem to have been very intimate & wish to form a stricter alliance, hollow eyes, large eyebrows, one colour all over the face & that between yellow & brown, whiskers reaching close to the mouth (really they come nearer the monkey than those you meet in Bond Street), a large cocked hat, a coat buttoned close round his neck & the lower part of the skirts [of the coat] just sufficient to reach the most prominent part of him, a waistcoat of dimity or jean, nankeen pantaloons and a pair of jack boots. Nearly the whole of them wear boots although there has not been a drop of rain these two months. Every boy of twelve years of age must have an enormous cocked hat to strut about with. You can have no idea how ridiculous some of them look moving (I cannot call it walking) along the streets. The inhabitants of Madrid are not all like those I have been describing but I think more than half of them are. There are some good-looking men who dress in the English fashion with the exception of the cocked hat. I do not see so many monks & friars here as at Lisbon.

The Spanish women are much handsomer than the men. I have not been in company with any but those in the house I am in, therefore am not capable of giving you so good a description of them as many can. They dress more elegantly than the English. They wear no bonnet or hat as it never rains here in summer but all wear something thrown over their heads & held with their left hand. They wear no trains to their dresses which are generally of black silk with silk cords hanging from the waist. You may tell their rank in a great measure by the handkerchief over their heads as they are universal, from the finest lace veil to the dish cloth. All the lower orders wear an immense lump of hair twisted round & tied with a gaudy ribbon. This furnishes them with their chief amusement. They sit upon the ground almost the whole day twisting and untwisting their hair – I have seen them drop asleep over it, awake, begin again, fall asleep & so on for twenty or thirty times together.

Everything manufactured here is much worse and double the price that it is in England. Their cutlery is infamous & most of their earthenware is very clumsy. Glass is much better & cheaper than in England. The lower class dress all their food in earthen pots, charcoal is universally used.

Madrid is not a fourth part of the size of London. There are very superb gates at the entrances to the city. On one side is a parade with several rows of trees reaching the whole length of it. It is crowded at dusk with Spanish ladies & gentlemen & English, Spanish & Portuguese officers both afoot & on horseback.

The manner in which the Spaniards get in their harvest has been very interesting to me. In England you can scarcely comprehend the meanings of the various passages in Oriental writings, particularly the Scriptures, as 'Thou shalt not muzzle the ox that treadeth out the corn' & alluding to Egypt. When they begin to cut the corn they never think of rain, as it never rains in the season for two or three months together. They reap it as we do. Their carts have a bag under them that holds a great deal and are all drawn by mules or oxen. The ox is the principal draught animal here. The harness is

'East View of Badajoz from a hill 1¼ [miles] distant.' A sketch by George Hennell. (See Letter I, page 11, for reference numbers.)

The Third Division escalading the Castle of Badajoz; a contemporary print (*National Army Museum*)

One of the forts at Salamanca sketched by George Hennell

The battle of Salamanca. Wellington watching the attack of the Fourth
Division; a post-war reconstruction of the scene by William Heath
(*National Army Museum*)

simply a piece of wood for two, fastened to the horns.[1] Each village has a smooth place near it and they lay the corn in a circle of about 16 yards in diameter and then two beasts draw a heavy door with pieces of flint placed in the wood about 2 inches asunder. The door is turned up in front that it may not push the corn before it and a man or woman, sometimes the whole family, sit in the middle while the oxen draw it round the ring. The corn is allowed to lie until the stem is as white and brittle as possible so that the machine threshes it and breaks the straws for chaff at the same time. They then lay it in heaps & keep throwing it in the air with a wooden fork until it is winnowed & then take it home.

You have no idea with what pleasure a party of Portuguese and Spaniards sit down to a mess of onions, garlic & cucumbers with oil, red pepper & salt. They eat enormous quantities of it. The olive & vineyards of Portugal are beautiful, many of them miles long. The olive tree is very like the willow and in vineyards in Spain (I have seen no olive trees in Spain yet) the vines are planted about one yard asunder & grow a foot high, spreading 3 or 4 yards. Fields are covered with them as with corn in England.

> Yours &c.
> G.H.

---

[1] Assistant Commissary August Schaumann makes the harnessing arrangement rather clearer: 'The draught bullocks are very large animals in this part of the world; they are also docile and fine to look upon. They are harnessed by means of a wooden yoke, which is fastened behind their horns and attached to the axle by leather straps.' (A. Schaumann, *On the Road with Wellington*, Ed: A. M. Ludovici, 1924, p. 9.)

LETTER VI

Madrid, 1st Sept. 1812.

DEAR BROTHERS,

Yesterday I saw the grand national amusement of the Spaniards. There was a grand bull fight in honour of Lord Wellington. Each of the officers had a ticket for the boxes – others paid 3/9d for admission to the boxes & 1/- for below.

I will now give you a minute description of it. The circus is close to the city. The inner circle is about 100 yards in diameter with a strong boarding fence about 6 feet high with a ledge about a foot from the ground for the fighters to step upon to spring over, & about two yards beyond that another the same. This goes all round except where the bull comes out & there are four pairs of folding gates forming the entrance into the circus and the ring. Between one of the folding gates there is a place where the bull comes out. Next to the 2nd partition are fourteen rows of seats one above another and above them a row of 120 boxes about the size of those at Covent Garden Theatre, holding 12 persons each. Above them is another row the same.

The fight began at ½ past 4 o'clock. The place was completely full. I arrived there just as Lord Wellington was going in. Six privates from each company were allowed to go below free. A sentinel was placed at each box to see that we went into the right one. The master of the ceremonies paraded in the ring with two attendants and two companies of Spanish soldiers. They paraded once or twice round the ring, then formed line and drove all [the spectators] over the first boarding. After clearing the ring they formed line in the centre, then filed off by twos till they came to the boarding. Then one man went one way, one another, leaving a man every three yards facing outwards. The trumpet sounded. They all jumped over immediately and remained with fixed bayonets.

Then entered 6 Spaniards on horseback having hats with brims 1 yard in diameter, a lance 16 feet long & about 2 inches thick – the spear[head] about 4 inches long and one broad – & gaily dressed in boots which, I believe, had iron in them. Then followed two cavaliers – the fighters with swords – & then 16 men with cloaks of different colours and all glaring, such as scarlet, crimson, &c., with cocked hats and were tightly dressed for running. They marched across the ring & bowed to Lord Wellington. Four of the horsemen went out & the rest remained. The footmen took off their hats.

The trumpet sounded (a shout). Out came the bull running wild about the ring. The cloakmen now ran past him, throwing out their cloaks, keeping hold of one corner. The bull immediately dashes at it. If a man is very near the bull he leaves his cloak & springs over the railings. The bull in two minutes came to one of the horsemen who immediately raised his spear under his right arm, grasping it firm, & there waited. The bull dashed at him with its head close to the ground in order to toss him but was received with his lance in the neck between the shoulders (the place always aimed at) which diverted the bull from the horse. The footmen then threw a cloak close to his nose which he dashed at. This is done to direct his attention from the horseman. The footmen kept constantly exasperating him in this way and he was frequently at their heels. They then dropped the cloak 3 or 4 yards from the boards. This stopped the bull & gave the man time to leap over. The horsemen did not go into the middle of the ring but waited at the edge for each attack. The bull in five minutes made another attack on the horseman and was received in the same manner as at first but he turned round and closed with the horse and tossed him several times before they could be parted. The horse had his hind thigh torn about three inches deep and 8 or 9 inches in length and a wound in the fore leg. The hind leg was in a few minutes a mass of gore with the loose flesh hanging about & the poor animal limping (cheering). When this had lasted about a quarter of an hour the trumpet sounded & the footmen appeared without their cloaks with a dart in each hand. This is a stick about $\frac{3}{4}$ of an inch thick and 1 yard long, tipped with iron about 6 inches from the point and has paper wrapped round it. They enticed the bull to fly at them; they then slipped nimbly on one side and drove both darts to a depth of 3 inches into his shoulder. After driving it straight in, the weight makes it fall close to his side. The dart always remains quite as far in, which makes the sticks fly about. In another two minutes another drove two more in. The blood by this time was running from every part of the bull's shoulder very fast. He moved close to the boarding & stood still a minute. The brutes drove another dart in near the tail. He ran about, shaking himself with pain which must have caused ten times more. Two more darts were stuck in (whenever a dart was stuck in there was a shout). This lasted about ten minutes. The trumpet blew. In came a cavalier with crimson silk over a stick about a yard long with which he went close to the bull, enticing him by waving the silk – the bull always dashes at the silk. The cavalier then takes his aim & if the bull comes sufficiently close to him he strikes him in the neck at the moment the bull is in the act of tossing, which forces the sword much further into the body than the man could do. The 2nd time the bull flew at him he thrust his sword in half a yard. The bull ran furiously about the ring with the sword in him. One of the men took hold of the sword & tried to push it in further but it was against a bone. The cavalier procured another sword &, after passing once or twice, drove it into the neck of the bull up to the handle. The bull then staggered and fell. One of the footmen then drove a dagger between the horns and killed it, the cavalier walking in triumph towards Lord Wellington and wiping his sword. The trumpet sounded. In came 3 mules finely decorated & a man behind with the wood the traces were to be fixed to, to which the bull was immediately fixed by the horns and drawn out at full gallop amidst the plaudits of the assembly. The horse that was wounded in the thigh was kept walking about to prevent his getting stiff.

The moment the gates closed others were opened & in came another bull. He dashed at a horseman (not the wounded one) & was struck with the lance, but he closed & gave the horse two or three gores just under the belly & one in the leg. The horseman was thrown but the footmen enticed the bull away with their cloaks whilst he mounted again. The bull then attacked the other horse, was received with the lance & pushed off. The footmen teased the bull with their cloaks as before. The horse that was gored in the belly had about 20 lbs weight of his entrails hanging down $\frac{1}{2}$ a yard. The man never offered to dismount. The English officers began to hiss. The man dismounted. In a minute he mounted again & spurred the poor animal (the weight continually increasing) to another attack, its entrails swinging about and limping with the wound in its foot. The English officers began hissing & crying 'No! No!' The brute mistook it, I suppose, for applause for he looked about him smiling. The rest of the audience was applauding. He dismounted & immediately remounted & spurred in again to the attack. The English increased their signs of disapprobation when he dismounted again & was going to mount when a man came in and prevented him. The horse after being two minutes longer in the ring with his entrails out was led out. The other horse was in a shocking state. The bull then flew at the wounded horse; another came in. The bull was received with the lance but closed and gave it a wound in the belly. This horse continued in the ring the whole of the fight. Darts were introduced as before & this was killed much as the first.

There were 6 more killed. One was worried by dogs & after they had been teasing him for some time a fellow, as coolly as possible, ran his sword in between the ribs as far as the handle. The last two were killed much the same as the others but, not being quite so fierce, the arrows were made with crackers all the way up, about twenty on each, lighted so that when the dart was driven in it set fire to them. Two of the bulls leaped in agony over the fence 6 feet high.

It lasted till 8 o'clock. No men (brutes I would say) were hurt. The stabbing the bull with the sword is esteemed the most dangerous part & the men showed great dexterity but the bulls always fly at the silk not the man.

Thus ended this scene of blood. This is having in perfection what Windham advocated &, it will be recollected, got a majority in its favour in the House of Commons to encourage the spirit of the lower classes.[1] These are the men (who delight in this scene) who seldom fail to run away when attacked by the French.

I have given a full description of this, for I shall see no more I

[1] William Windham (1750–1810), politician and twice Secretary of State for War, 'one of the most charming, scholarly and eloquent, but also the least competent, of all men to have held that office'. There is nothing in his published speeches to suggest that he favoured the introduction of bull-fighting into Britain but on two occasions (1802 and 1804) he successfully opposed bills to stop bull-baiting. His ostensible grounds were that it was a poor man's sport and no more cruel than the rich man's fox hunting. He later successfully opposed a bill designed to restrict cruelty to animals of all kinds.

assure you. Remember I was an eye-witness, therefore you may believe what I write. *The half of the audience were ladies and they applauded it.*

Yours &c.
G.H.

LETTER VII

Madrid, 19th Sept. 1812.

DEAR BROTHERS,

The officers who are in this place have excellent quarters – in general a handsome suite of 2 or 3 rooms fitted up very elegantly, painted & much higher than the generality of those in England. We have a great deal of duty to do here besides which I have to drill twice a day so that I have but little time to myself. There is no regiment [which] drills their officers so much as ours & for that reason it is the best disciplined in the service.[1]

One of the officers who was present at the capture of Fort La China[2] gave me a very good French sword which I wear, a gun also of which our armourer has made me a very good fowling piece. There is a great quantity of game within a league of this place. An officer belonging to us one day shot a deer & five brace of pheasants – no game laws here.

On Saturday I was in orders to conduct a party of prisoners (two

---

[1] John Cooke, who joined the Forty Third as an ensign in 1809, described the way in which young officers learned their business. 'When an officer entered this corps it was an invariable custom to send him to drill with a squad composed of peasants from the plough tail or other raw recruits, first learning the facings, marchings and companies' evolutions. That being completed, the officer put on cross-belts and pouch and learned the firelock exercise; then again he marched with the same : and when it was considered that the whole was perfect, with and without arms, they began to skirmish in extended files, and last of all learned the duties of a sentry, and to fire ball cartridge at a target. The officer, after all this, was not considered clear of the adjutant until he could put a company through the evolutions by a word of command which he had practised in the ranks. It generally took him six months in summer at four times a day (an hour each period) to perfect him in all he had to learn.' (*Memoirs of the Late War: the personal narrative of Captain Cook* [sic], 43rd L.I.Regt. 1831, pp. 32–3.)

[2] La China fort was more usually known as the Retiro. It was based on the buildings of the Buen Retiro china factory in the Retiro Park in Madrid.

days march) to the Escorial. I started on Sunday morning with 219 men, 14 officers & 8 deserters & had an escort of 20 rank & file & two sergeants. If you had seen me on the road outside Madrid ordering the party to load you would have cried 'Bless me! How consequential George is'. I treated the officers with familiarity & allowed three Germans to sleep in the house with me & the other 11 (Frenchmen) to cook their victuals & remain with me till dusk. We halted at [Las] Rozas & put the men in a chapel & the officers in a gallery belonging to it. They asked me to sleep in the place but I did not think it prudent. I ordered the sentinels to keep a sharp look out, which they did & about 12 o'clock the officers were trying to force the door behind, on which the sentry fired but did not wound any but it silenced them for the night. I delivered them up safe to a man at the Escorial & from there the Adjutant General was going to send me to Salamanca but I got off. The officer before me lost 20 & had less men with a larger escort, another lost a colonel.

There is a fair in Madrid at present. All the inhabitants (rich & poor) have to dispose of is placed at the door. If you wish for a portrait of our Saviour I can procure one of what age and shape you please either in the arms of His Mother, with His head shaved like a monk, or on a white horse with a Spanish dragoon's sword killing green dragoons, or ordering a monk to draw 5 or 6 men out of hell by their hair. In short it would be a vain attempt to describe the number of absurd situations I have seen Him placed in & in pictures very well painted.

I witnessed a funeral a few days since. The face of the corpse is always uncovered & they are never buried in a coffin. The fingers are locked in each other over the breast & a pair of wax lights between the longest fingers to resemble a cross. They take the corpse into a church & place it on a pedestal & the priests say as many masses as the friends of the deceased can afford to pay for.

You ask how it is no more Spaniards were killed on the 22nd July. There are 12 Spaniards attached to each regiment and it was among them, I suppose, the two killed & four wounded were. There was no Spanish regiment with us on the 22nd July except Don Julian's Guerrillas of the Armies in Valencia,[1] and of Ballasteros you know as

---

[1] There had been 3,360 Spanish troops under Don Carlos de España at the battle of Salamanca. Don Julian Sanchez commanded only one regiment, the Lanceros de Castilla (not Valencia), which had previously been a

much as I do. The only Spanish troops I have seen are the guerrillas and 2 or 3 Spanish regiments when I first entered Spain. I hear great numbers are to be raised and proclamations are stuck up in abundance but I saw nothing like it. The inhabitants do town duty here such as guarding the post office, &c. I firmly believe that if Lord Wellington were offered another Light Division in lieu of the whole Spanish force (except the guerrillas) he would not hesitate a moment.[1]

YOURS &c.
G.H.

---

guerrilla band. The small number of Spanish casualties was due to their place in Wellington's line of battle rather than to any backwardness on their part.

[1] Five days after this letter was written Wellington was offered the chief command of all the Spanish armies by the *Cortes*. He accepted it as soon as he obtained permission to do so from London but it made little or no difference in his relationship with either the Spanish government or their generals.

LETTER VIII

Madrid, 16th October 1812.

DEAR BROTHERS,

As a soldier I have much to learn. I am still at drill &, as I see the propriety of it, it gives me pleasure. There is a park just here (Casa del Campo) with a vast quantity of game in which I shoot when at leisure. The weather this last week has been very wet & cold. If we have a winter's campaign our noses will have a fine complexion.

Four or five of the regiments have subscribed a day's pay each month to be given to the poor in soup. A play (The Revenge & Mayor of Garrett) was performed by the officers of the 95th, 43rd, 94th & 47th regiments for the benefit of the poor. It produced 250 dollars. The poor are very numerous here & many are most wretched objects. In the great streets you are stopped every 5 or 6 yards & frequently by 6 or 7 at once. There are no Poor Laws here and I have not heard of any hospitals for their reception. The whole of them seem naturally idle. If any are ill they are exposed in the streets and frequently nearly naked. I have seen children five or six years of age lying on the pavement with scarcely one ounce of flesh on their arms & making a piteous moaning. After dark they lie down against a door doubled almost together that the little clothing they have may cover the whole of them – some sleeping, others crying. Last night I counted eight doors with one in each.

19th October 1812. It is not improbable that we march tomorrow. At least we expect one soon. I hear the siege of Burgos is turned into a blockade.[1] I am in pretty good order for marching, never had better

---

[1] There was no idea of turning the siege of Burgos into a blockade. The last letter received at Hill's headquarters from Wellington envisaged the probability of having to abandon the operation altogether in view of the reports of the French advance from Valencia on Madrid. As Wellington wrote, 'It is absolutely necessary that I should raise this siege and proceed to the south, and I shall do so as soon as the weather holds up a little.' (WD

health in my life. Tea & sugar in good order[1] – 2 horses &c. We have had 8 or 10 stolen from our regiment within the last month.

       Yours &c.
       G.H.

---

ix 485.) He did not mention that, as a last resort, a mine was being dug under the defences and that it would soon be ready to be sprung. The mine was fired and a last assault made on 18 October. It was repulsed and on 20 October preparations for abandoning the siege were begun. By that time the French were beginning to press in from the north and the retreat began on the night of the 21st.

[1] A typical infantry subaltern's campaigning kit was described by Robert Blakeney, a lieutenant in the Twenty Eight Foot. 'Our little stock of tea, sugar and brandy was carefully hoarded [with] a little tin kettle, which also acted the part of a teapot; *two* cups and saucers (in case of company), two spoons, two forks, two plates of the same metal, a clasp knife, a small soup-tureen, which on fortunate occasions acted as punch-bowl but never for soup.' (*A Boy in the Peninsular War*, Ed: J. Sturgis, 1899, p. 209.) In addition there would be a blanket, a change of underclothes and a boat-cloak.

LETTER IX

DEAR BROTHERS,

We left Madrid about a week since & came here, 5 leagues from it, on the 26th. 27th marched to Arganda, a long day's march. We there learned that Soult was only 5 leagues from us & Gen. Hill was 3 leagues between us and him.[1] There was good wine in the village & the inhabitants did not give our soldiers a little. Most of them were merry, some quite drunk – my servant was quite gone.

At ½ past 9 at night the order came for marching. A scene of this kind is very curious. We do not know but that the enemy are within half a mile of us, frequently they are. In 5 or 10 minutes the soldiers are all accoutred & formed in their companies, the officers busy in seeing the baggage is well packed. In a quarter of an hour the regiments are formed in due order. It would do those good who suppose British soldiers have any fear to have been among them last night. The conversation among the men is interspersed with the most horrid oaths declaring what they will do with the fellow they lay hands on. What they intend to get in plunder, hoping they will stand a chance that they may split two at once. Then someone more expert at low wit than his companions draws a ludicrous picture of

---

[1] Soult's army was in the area Aranjuez–Fuenteduenas on 26–7 October. Hill had his forward posts facing them across the Tagus but withdrew his infantry to the Tajuna during the night 27–8. He was prepared to defend this line until he received, early on 29 October, orders from Wellington to retreat since the northern part of the army was heavily out-numbered in the position it had taken up near Valladolid.

On the extreme right of Hill's line there was a rearguard action at the Puenta Larga, where the road from Aranjuez to Madrid crosses the Tajuna, but by the evening of that day, 30 October, the whole of Hill's corps, less the rearguard, was concentrated near Madrid. They made their retreat from there without being molested.

a Frenchman with a bayonet stuck in him or something of the kind, which raises a loud and general laugh. Others describe what they have achieved in this way. In short, it is more like a fair time than the beginning of a bloody action. They marched off & forgot the evening & for amusement by the way commenced their wit upon each other with grossness & sometimes point hardly to be exceeded. As they grow tired they begin to swear at the country & the inhabitants. As they get more so, at soldiering & the commissaries & when nearly exhausted there is little said except now & then a faint dispute about distance, &c. But when they arrive, if they can get wine, all their troubles are instantly forgotten & songs & hoarse laughs resound through the place. We left Arganda at 10 o'clock and arrived here at daylight, very cold & much fatigued. We are all ready to turn out at a minute's warning. Lord Wellington is expected soon if he is not here now.

[The end of this letter appears to be missing]

3 Retreat to Portugal

In October 1812 Wellington found himself in 'the worst military situation I was ever in'. Having divided his army to besiege Burgos in the north while holding the line of the Tagus south of Madrid, he was threatened by superior forces on both fronts. He started retreating from Burgos on 21 October and the southern corps, commanded by Rowland Hill, evacuated Madrid on 1 November.

Despite some anxious moments on the northern withdrawal the whole allied army, 65,000 British, Portuguese and Spaniards, was united near Salamanca by 8 November. The two French columns which had pursued them joined soon afterwards led by King Joseph with Marshals Soult and Jourdan and 85,000 strong. On 15 November Wellington offered them battle on the ground where he had defeated Marmont in the previous July but Soult, who was in tactical command of the French, fumbled his opportunity to the fury of his entire army. As a very angry Jourdan wrote, 'the opportunity was lost for putting right in a single day all the misfortunes of the campaign'.

The last stage of the allied retreat, from Salamanca to Ciudad Rodrigo, was a miserable affair. The weather was appalling and, except for beef which accompanied the army on the hoof, no rations were issued since the Quartermaster General, Colonel James Willoughby Gordon, sent all the supplies back by the wrong road. Fortunately the French only pressed the rearguard on one day and were fought off without much difficulty. Nevertheless the British part of the army, 53,648 strong, lost 2,098 men missing and had an addition of 1,537 to their already large sick list in the five day journey.

LETTER X

Salamanca, 12th November.

By this you will see how completely I was mistaken in supposing we were going to Valencia.[1] Rumours are as numerous here as in England and for the future I shall send nothing but what I see.

On the 28th our company was for the outlying piquet. The whole division lay accoutred in the streets all night. Next day at eight o'clock in the morning the route came to march immediately. It was very wet. We marched out of the village and halted an hour until the whole of the sick & baggage were in advance. We then marched in rain continuing until two o'clock &, just at dark, arrived at Madrid. We marched all round the city & at 9 o'clock arrived at a hill about 4 miles on this side Madrid. We then found Gen. Hill's army & the 3rd & 4th Divisions. As we came near Madrid the Retiro was burning.[2] It was a very cold night. Not half of us had tents. With a piece of damp wood I had the good fortune to get I made a fire & gave a gala to two other officers of tea & mutton chops & then lay down to sleep with my blanket & a boat cloak over me.

---

[1] The letter containing this supposition is missing. It was probably in the missing portion of Letter IX. King Joseph's army had fallen back to Valencia during August. There it had joined Marshal Suchet's Army of Aragon and Valencia (32,000 strong) and that in its turn had been joined by Soult's Army of the South (47,000), which had evacuated Andalusia as a result of the battle of Salamanca. Since the allied corps around Madrid was only 43,000 strong, including 12,000 Spaniards, an attack on Valencia would have been a very dangerous move and Wellington never contemplated undertaking it. In the event Joseph and Soult were advancing on Madrid with 61,000 men.

[2] The Retiro fort was blown up on 30 October to prevent the French from using it again. The fire Hennell saw was probably the army's surplus stores being burnt to prevent them from falling into the hands of the enemy.

The next day our division marched back to the gates of Madrid & lay there all day.[1] At night time we took up our position on the hills & found all the other divisions had marched & we were to bring up the rear. At 3 o'clock next morning I was called up to the baggage & continued advancing before the division a league or two for 3 or 4 days.

The French entered Madrid the day after we left. We then kept retreating regularly, the French keeping at a respectful distance (a league or more off). 3 nights ago we halted on a hill about a mile from the spot [Garçia Hernandez] where the Germans cut up the French in Marmont's retreat after the battle of the 22nd July.[2] It was very cold. Few of the officers had either anything to eat or to wrap themselves up in. I had both a blanket, meat & tea with milk from my goat, which supplies me morning & night, so that I fared well & lay me down and slept as comfortable as ever I did in my life. About 11 o'clock it began to rain hard & did so most part of the night. The morning presented a scene as complete as you can conceive. There was not a camp up in the division. Colonels, majors, captains, all wet through. I was very little so though my cap took up rather an unfortunate position as it was half full of water. Fires were soon lighted & we got round them joking over our night's amusement, each giving a description of his particular adventure. Some said that on awakening they found their elbows in a puddle, others a stream running down their backs, &c., &c.

We marched in about an hour to Alba de Tormes and waited under a wall (it rained all the morning) till the town was told off for quarters. We then received orders from Lord Wellington to march immediately to him in Salamanca, 4 leagues off. We halted $1\frac{1}{2}$ miles from the wood where the battle of the 22nd of July was fought. We stayed there all day & at night received an order to march at 4 o'clock to Salamanca. We arrived today. Lord Wellington, Gen. Hill and a great number of Spanish troops with the whole of our army are here.

Yesterday morning we were exactly in our old position & Soult,

---

[1] This counter-march was necessitated by riots in Madrid. The Light Division returned to the gates of the city and two companies of the Fifty Second were sent into the streets to restore order.

[2] See p. 31, note 1.

who had joined Marmont's army,[1] was exactly in the place Marmont occupied on the 22nd July. Gen. Hill on the other side of the Tormes. We lay under the hill until 3 o'clock in the afternoon & then came in again.

This has been rather a fatiguing retreat to our animals & not very pleasant to ourselves but by no means so disagreeable as you may imagine. If we are well and get a comfortable meal we are repaid for our disagreeables. You in England have no idea of the enjoyment of a cup of good tea with a chop or steak in our fingers sitting on the ground on a fine morning after a rainy night. Our troubles are horses and mules dying, getting sore backs & losing things on the march. Our baggage has been packing & unpacking 3 or 4 times a day & half the times in the dark. I have a little, if not my share of this. My mare has a sore back & I have lost a blanket & bag. One of our officers lost three mules in four days, others 2 & many one each. I never was in better health in my life, though I have slept in the fields every night but two the last fortnight.

YOURS &c.
G.H.

---

[1] Marmont having been seriously wounded at Salamanca, his army was commanded by General Joseph Souham. This force, the 'Army of Portugal', which had followed Wellington from Burgos, joined Soult's column (see page 57, note 1) east of Salamanca on 11 November.

LETTER XI

DEAR BROTHERS,

On the 14th inst. at 10 o'clock in the morning we were ordered to march to the very same spot we lay on the 22nd July. We waited there the whole day with our army in the old position & the enemy in a very strong one alongside of us. There was a cannonade in the afternoon; it was very wet then & at night. We fully expected another battle the next day but they moved forward [i.e. towards Ciudad Rodrigo and Wellington's line of retreat] & we marched at 10 o'clock towards Ciudad Rodrigo. I was completely wet thro' before I was a league from Salamanca & the road was excessively bad. The Light Division was in the rear. We marched until dark & halted at the entrance to a wood. Here we were all completely wet to the skin, very cold & most of the baggage soaked through. It was an hour before the spot was fixed, as we were last & the enemy were close behind. My mare's back was so sore that she could carry nothing; my pony was therefore obliged to carry all the baggage & I walked. Conceive my situation the hour we stood still with no other expectation but that of lying down in wet clothes exposed to the rain. A friend gave me a place in his tent where I got some tea & a complete change of clothes from my box & in which I slept comfortably.

Next morning at daylight it rained hard & was excessively cold. I believe one half the steps the troops took we were over our ankles in mud & water. In the middle of the day it cleared up and was fine. We halted at sun set in a wood with the ground soaked in rain. Every hour of the march I expected the pony to fall dead for it had not had anything to eat since we left Salamanca except the little grass he found in the old position. The batmen[1] were ordered to go about $\frac{1}{2}$ a

---

[1] A batman was not, as in the twentieth century, a soldier servant but a soldier detailed to look after the baggage animals.

mile into a village for straw but we heard the French were there. Tonight we have procured some chopped straw. The greater part of the way the poor things took was up to their knees in mud.

Next morning (16th November) I was awoke by the rain on my blanket. At daylight I was ordered to go forward with a sergeant to collect the stores and sick & to halt the former on the other side of a river [the Huebra] a league in advance. I passed the 7th Division and its baggage. As I came down the hill to a river the French attacked our division. Our men had had no bread or biscuit since they left Salamanca. I went on with the baggage & found two of our cars at dark at a village where the baggage halted. My Portuguese boy & goat were left behind & I have not seen him since. I there learned that the French were in great force. Our cavalry & theirs skirmished & three of our companies were ordered out for the same purpose, mine (No. 8) was one of them. As our skirmishers came in a cannonade opened upon them. The French likewise came out of the wood & presented themselves in front of the 7th Division & took most of their baggage. Of course, being with our baggage and not a league before, [I] was near being taken. Had I found bread on the road I must inevitably have been a prisoner for the women & sick belonging to our regiment, who were a short distance behind, were taken.[1] The women they took some of (the handsome ones) & let others go. All this day it rained excessively hard. I lay down after getting some rum & meat on a wet mattress with a wet blanket for a covering. It was the worst night I ever spent. Next day I came up with our stores and slept with them as our baggage was at Rodrigo, 2 leagues further. I procured something to eat but had only a tarpaulin to cover me. It was a frosty night & so cold I could not sleep $\frac{1}{2}$ an hour together. Next morning our regiment passed when I joined & went to Rodrigo; then crossed the river to a convent $\frac{1}{2}$ a league off on the banks of it.[2] The convent was very filthy & had half its roof off. I slept out that night as it was fine but it rained in the morning so got into the convent with the men. For accommodation it was little

---

[1] The capture of the women and sick belonging to the Forty Third is not recorded by any of the other letters and accounts written by members of the regiment. It seems probable that Hennell got hold of a distorted story and that the captives belonged to a battalion in the Seventh Division which lost a substantial amount of baggage.

[2] The convent of La Caridad.

better than a pig-stye. My eyes were so much affected by the smoke I could scarcely see the next day. Next day we passed the same, very wet, & the night was worse for the smoke was intolerable. Yesterday we arrived here at ten o'clock, very wet & cold.

November 25th. You may recollect that in one of my letters I mentioned one of our officers having on the 22nd July been struck by a ball on his button and which lodged in his handkerchief. He was also slightly wounded at Badajoz. He was a very pleasant unassuming young man, Lieut. [George] Ridout was his name. Just after they crossed the river & formed column a 4-pounder shot took off his right foot & it was a day & a half before it could be amputated. He was brought here & the next day a mortification ensued in the other foot from excessive cold & which destroyed him in 24 hours. I was one of the pall-bearers & saw him buried yesterday in the small breach by the side of the late Genl. Craufurd.[1]

Thus has ended my first campaign & after all the fatigues I have undergone have not even a slight cold. The loss of our regiment in this retreat has been between 20 & 30 killed & wounded.[2] Many of our men were with Sir John Moore & they say this from Salamanca was quite as bad only shorter.[3] In that they had plenty to eat & drink; in this they had neither bread nor biscuits owing, we suppose, to the neglect of the commissaries. The principal [Commissary] is discharged, & the rest are to be tried by court martial.[4] In Rodrigo

---

[1] Major General Robert Craufurd, the original commander of the Light Division, had been mortally wounded at the storm of Ciudad Rodrigo (19 January 1812), and was buried at the foot of the breach which his division had stormed.

[2] The loss of the Forty Third was one officer died of wounds, one sergeant killed, one officer (Lieutenant M. H. Baillie), one sergeant and ten rank and file wounded, three sergeants and twenty-two rank and file missing.

[3] Lieutenant Colonel William Gomm, Ninth Foot, who was in both retreats, wrote on 22 November 1812 that in that year, 'In some respects the hardships were greater, for on that occasion [La Coruña] the troops were generally under cover; but here the only resting place was a bleak swampy plain, with more temptation in it to watch than to sleep, and to look with impatience for the break of the following morning.' (*Letters & Memorials of Field Marshal Sir William Maynard Gomm* (1881), p. 290.)

[4] Two Assistants Commissary General attached to the cavalry were sent home for 'great neglect of duty' (one of them being subsequently reprieved). Three Commissariat Clerks, attached to the cavalry and Horse Artillery, were reprimanded but the Commissariat staff of the Light Division were

everything is excessively dear :– tea 4 dollars per lb; sugar 2/-;
butter 4/- lb.

Yours &c.
G.H.

---

not accused, although Captain Henry Booth, Forty Third, also wrote that
the division's Commissary 'is to be dismissed'. It was not the fault of the
Commissariat officers that the troops were without rations for three days
but that of Quartermaster General. Fortunately he returned sick to England
and did not return.

LETTER XII

DEAR BROTHERS,

I am now a rich man. I have 14 guineas in my pocket, nearly 4 months pay in arrears, 14 dollars bât & forage money due to me, my wardrobe in good order, two horses and my credit standing as high as any officer's in the regiment. I assure you very few of us have any money when a fresh supply arrives. I made a right honourable officer of our regiment stare a few days since when he was wondering how he should procure a dollar to go to the Spanish general's ball at Rodrigo.[1] I lent him a guinea. In this way I have gained many friends. Besides, having money preserves me from many of the mortifications I see others endure by spending their money as soon as they get it. In addition to this it affords me the means of keeping up the respectability of my appearance which is necessary as our regiment is always near head quarters.

My comic powers have had a fine opportunity of displaying themselves as you will see by the playbills enclosed. The Prince of Orange[2] enquired after me & honoured me with a polite bow as he entered Gallegos the last play day.

I have given half a dollar for twelve sheets of writing paper and shall fill them with accounts of the next campaign. I am now studying military tactics & have no doubt I shall soon have an opportunity of putting them in practice, for as soon as we have done acting comedies here, there is little doubt we shall have to act in [the] tragedy of the country. Lord Fitzroy Somerset told us a day or two

---

[1] The Spanish General was Don Luis Wimpffen, a Swiss by birth, who had been appointed Spanish Quartermaster General at Wellington's head-quarters. The 'right honourable officer of our regiment' was, presumably, Ensign the Hon. Charles Monck.

[2] An extra A.D.C. to Wellington.

LIGHT DIVISION THEATRE.

GALLEGOS.

On Thursday, the 4th. February 1813.

WILL BE PERFORMED THE COMEDY OF

THE RIVALS.

M E N.

Sir Anthony Absolute,	Lieut. Patenson, 43d. Regt.
Captain Absolute,	Capt. Beckwith, 95th. Regt.
Faulkland,	Lieut. Pemberton, 95th. Regt.
Sir Lucius O'Trigger,	Lieut. Cox, 95th. Regt.
Acres,	Capt. Cator Royal Artillery,
David,	Lieut. Hennel, 43d. Regt.
Fag,	Lieut. Havelock, 43d. Regt.
Coachman,	Lieut. Hamilton, 95th. Regt.

W O M E N.

Mrs. Malaprop,	Capt. Hobkirk. 43d. Regt,
Lydia Languish,	Lt. Hble. C. Gore, 43d. Regt.
Julia,	Lieut. Lord C. Spencer, 95th. Regt.
Lucy,	Lieut. Freer, 43d.

AFTER WHICH A VARIETY OF COMIC SONGS.

VIVAT WELLINGTON.

[PRINTED AT FRENEDA.]

since that he thought Lord Wellington would never go to a siege again without the Light Division.[1]

YOURS &c.
G.H.

---

[1] Wellington had written as early as 21 September, when the siege of Burgos was going badly, that 'If I had here the troops who have stormed so often [i.e. the Third and Light Divisions], I should not have lost a fourth of the number.' In fact, when Wellington had to undertake another siege (San Sebastian) he did not call on either of his 'storming divisions' but later sent to them for parties of volunteers 'to show the Fifth Division how to mount a breach'.

4 'In Fortune's Way'

Even though the campaign of 1812 had ended with Wellington's army back on the Portuguese frontier there were large advantages gained, not least the evacuation of southern Spain by the French. On 18 January Wellington received the *29ᵐᵉ Bulletin* which told of Napoleon's disaster in Russia and realized that the French in Spain would not be receiving any reinforcements and that they might be weakened by having to send drafts to the emperor's army in Germany. Within a month of hearing this news Wellington was telling London 'I propose to get in fortune's way. . . . I cannot have a better opportunity for trying the fate of a battle which, if the enemy should be unsuccessful, must oblige him to withdraw altogether.' He intended, in fact, to drive the French out of Spain. He had an army of 52,000 British and 28,000 Portuguese and such help, initially 12,000 men, as the Spaniards could give him.

King Joseph, with Marshal Jourdan as chief of staff, should have had 95,000 men to guard the Spanish-Portuguese frontier but Napoleon insisted that he send six divisions to assist the Army of the North in putting down the guerrillas in Biscay and Navarre. This meant that, while Wellington would start with a numerical superiority, he would be driving the French back on to reserves of 60,000 men. To win his decisive battle he must hustle King Joseph so fast that he would not be able to collect these reserves.

Joseph and Jourdan expected Wellington to advance from Ciudad Rodrigo on Salamanca as he had done in 1812 and made their dispositions accordingly. On 21 May 1813 an allied column, heavily shrouded in cavalry, did advance on this road but the bulk of Wellington's army had already crossed the Douro within Portugal and struck behind the French right flank. Soon all the allies were on the north bank advancing in four large columns to the north west. The most southerly column was commanded by Rowland Hill, the next by Wellington himself. Thomas Graham had the left column and on the extreme left were the available Spaniards. Constantly outflanked the French were forced to fall back day after day and had to abandon Burgos, which was still being repaired after the siege of 1812. By 20 June Joseph's army, without its reserves, had got back as far as Vitoria, within sixty-five miles of France. At a cost of only 201 casualties Wellington had advanced 300 miles in 29 days. The scene was set for the battle 'which, if the enemy is unsuccessful, must oblige him to withdraw altogether'.

LETTER XIII

Aldea Nueva de Figueira, 4 leagues, N.W. of
Salamanca, 30 May 1813.

DEAR BROTHERS,

Our division was reviewed by Lord Wellington & all his splendid staff with him on the 18th inst.[1] previous to marching. We made a good appearance. Our regiment mustered on the ground 80 per company, 10 comps to the regiment – 10 captains, 29 subalterns, few muster so many. Such a review in England would have been attended by crowds & here, tho' in great measure their prosperity depends upon it & there are several towns within 2 or 3 miles, not a single Spaniard or Portuguese came as a spectator.

On the 21st we marched. We have encamped ever since. Three nights ago we encamped on the banks of the Tormes, 1 league below Salamanca and halted. The next day most of us went into Salamanca, & although the French had only left the night before, the people were quite at their ease. The shops were all open as we left them.

Te Deum was performed at the cathedral. All the grandees were there. Lord Wellington was dressed in a grey frock coat, white handkerchief, an old sword & cock'd hat. Castaños & another Spanish general were by his side in full dress.

We have now halted here two days. Genl. Hill's army is 2 miles to our right. We have received no intelligence from the other side of the Douro yet. I caught a fine plate of fish in the river [Huebra] where the French drove our division in on the 17th November. How

---

[1] 'All the fashionables of the army were at the review this morning near Espeja [close to Ciudad Rodrigo] and a very fine sight it was. Between five and six thousand of the *élite* of ours, and of the Portuguese troops; the line near three-quarters of a mile long, two deep, and they marched in line near half a mile over rough and smooth, and then changed their front three times, and at last passed in review admirably. . . . the day was beautiful and the scene upon the whole very striking.' (*Journal of Judge Advocate Larpent* (3rd edn. 1854), p. 116.)

[69]

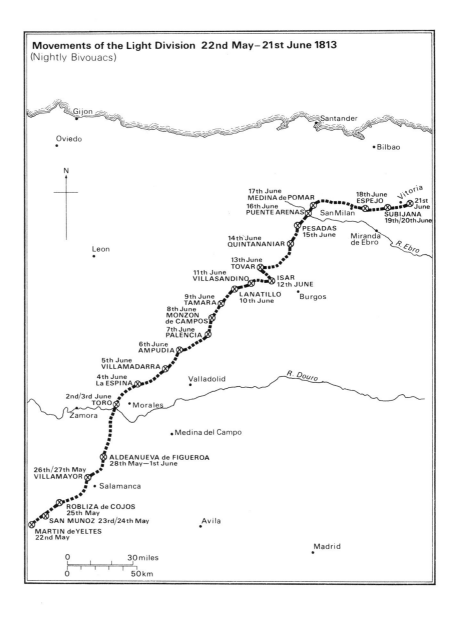

Movements of the Light Division 22nd May – 21st June 1813
(Nightly Bivouacs)

Gijon

Oviedo

Santander

• Bilbao

N

Vitoria

17th June
MEDINA de POMAR
16th June
PUENTE ARENAS

18th June
ESPEJO

21st
June

San Milan

SUBIJANA
19th/20th June

PESADAS
15th June

Miranda
de Ebro

R. Ebro

Leon

14th June
QUINTANANIAR

13th June
TOVAR

11th June
VILLASANDINO

ISAR
12th JUNE

LANATILLO
10th June

Burgos

9th June
TAMARA

8th June
MONZON
de CAMPOS

7th June
PALENCIA

6th June
AMPUDIA

5th June
VILLAMADARRA

4th June
La ESPINA

Valladolid

R. Douro

2nd/3rd June
TORO

• Morales

Zamora

• Medina del Campo

ALDEANUEVA de FIGUEROA
28th May—1st June

26th/27th May
VILLAMAYOR

• Salamanca

ROBLIZA de COJOS
25th May
SAN MUNOZ 23rd/24th May
MARTIN de YELTES
22nd May

• Avila

• Madrid

0   30 miles

0   50 km

differently I passed the road this time from the last. Now it is fine weather & good roads. Many spots I remember to have lost my shoes in or to have been getting upon a car to pass a slough.

I have just heard a few cavalry drove in Hill's piquets last night. They belonged to the Madrid army.[1]

Camp near Toro, 3rd June. Two thousand French came down to the place I last wrote from & then retired. We had to throw out our piquets & half a regiment as a support. They had 7,000 cavalry & we had only 1,000 with us.

Yesterday we marched from Aldea Nueva de Figueira to Toro, $7\frac{1}{2}$ leagues. We call 4 leagues a long march. Our regiment is such excellent order that only 2 men and 1 sergeant fell out on the march. The Hussar brigade (that has just come out) in the morning gave a fine introduction to the campaign. The French in Toro kept a very sharp look out. However, they (our cavalry) crossed the Douro at a very dangerous ford (they had 12 men drowned) & pursued the French very close.[2] The French supposed them to be Spanish or Portuguese cavalry & the general ordered 300 of his best cavalry to charge them in their usual furious way, which I before described. The Hussars waited until they were within 2 or 3 yards, perfectly steady, & then made full use of their spurs, broke them in an instant & literally cut them to pieces, for they have killed or taken prisoners nearly the whole of them – not 10 escaped. Our loss was not more than 10 killed &, I suppose, as many wounded. The poor fellows are cut up in every way – some their lips off, some their noses, backs, arms, heads cut in every direction. Don Julian [Sanchez] has sent in 40 more this morning.[3]

---

[1] This appears to have been a false alarm. The 'Madrid army' was the French Army of the Centre, the smallest of the armies facing Wellington.

[2] This episode occurred at the crossing of the Esla, a large tributary of the Douro. On 31 May the Hussar Brigade crossed the river which was in flood at a very difficult ford near Almendra with infantrymen of the Fifty First and Brunswick Light Infantry clinging to their stirrups. About twenty-five of the infantry were swept away and drowned. The hussars captured a near-by French piquet who were cooking their breakfast.

[3] This action did not, as Hennell suggests, take place immediately after the crossing of the Esla but two days later at Morales, six miles east of Toro. The Tenth Hussars, with the Eighteenth in support, charged two French dragoon regiments and broke them. More than two hundred Frenchmen were captured. The Tenth lost one officer and one trooper killed, twelve wounded and two officers and three other ranks, captured.

They have blown up two arches of the bridge [at Toro] in a very complete manner & had fortified it in such a manner as to make it impossible to force a passage. Toro is on the edge of the hill over the river. It is a rugged precipice about as high as Greenwich Hill & steeper. A strong fort was constructed on the top by the French. Our division passed the river, which is as broad as the Thames at London. It took my baggage horse (which is 12 hands high) up to the belly. The men passed the bridge by ladders.[1] We began at sunrise & finished about twelve at noon. Our brigade passed first & we did not wait for the other so that we arrived here at 10 o'clock & had an excellent breakfast.

Gluttons in England have tried many methods of making their food most relishing. I will give you a recipe which I have tried. First: Sound 8 bugle horns, 4 yards from his tent 1 hour before daybreak: desire the servant to draw up the peg of his tent & pack it up. & if he does not dress in 5 minutes the stars will find him naked. Let him then march, or be on duty (with only a small piece of bread), till 11 or 12 o'clock & then lay him down on a mattress in a pure cool tent with tea, bread, Irish butter, milk hot from the goat and a beef steak fired in water (which we call good). Then let him lie down to sleep for 2 or 3 hours, have his dinner, smoke his pipe or cigar and drink his grog or wine. As he turns out of his tent in the morning, he will most likely say 'Confound soldiering' and before the day is out cry out, 'Really, campaigning is very pleasant.' But remember that I have always been mounted & have had tea, coffee, sugar & milk by me with excellent help or perhaps my tone might have been somewhat different.

The whole of the army, except Genl. Hill's division [2nd] & some Spanish troops, is now on the right bank of the Douro. I have not heard where the 6th Division is. It is near by, I suppose. We met Lord Wellington going down to the bridge as we came up. The children called 'Viva' as we passed Toro & so did some old women but the men (brutes) stood perfectly unconcerned & paid about the same attention as an old cobbler smoking his pipe does to a mail

---

[1] John Cooke's description of the crossing at Toro was: 'The soldiers descended by ladders placed close together, communicating by planks thrown across to the steps of the opposite ladders, by which the men again ascended.' All accounts other than Hennell's say that only one arch of the bridge had been blown.

coach passing through a market-place in England. The priests bow & smile to you, saying 'God be with you'. I think about ⅓rd may wish as they say & have little doubt but the remainder would as soon give you some curses.

Toro is a small town with a mud wall round it. Valladolid is about 9 leagues from us. The French have gone there. Burgos is about 18 more. We do not expect to have anything to do until we get there. Until a day or two before we marched the weather was as cold as in England or more so.

I forgot to say a squadron saw a piquet [of] about 40 infantry 2 miles off. They started at full gallop, the French running as fast as they could. The race lasted 2 or 3 hours, only 3 escaped. The Hussars had none killed or wounded. It was a very fine race.[1]

There is an abundance of grapes. Vines, cherry, walnut & peach trees on the bank of the Douro, but none ripe, & some beautiful fields of corn. What would an Englishman make of this country? They would be able to supply half the continent with corn & fruit but water would be very much wanted for canals & manufactories. Whatever may be said of the climate of England, it is without [question] the finest country for enjoyment. Here you are sick of fine days.

Ampudia, June 6th. 4 lea[gues] W. of Palencia. We came here today & it is very probable may march again tonight. We are moving in 3 columns, 6th & 7th Divisions on our right, 3rd, 4th & Light in the centre, 1st & 5th on our left. Genl. Hill's 2nd [Division], a reserve to support either. You perceive we have left Valladolid on our right. Nothing has happened since my last. The French keep retiring & collecting about 3, 4 or 5 leagues in advance of us. Our cavalry are in their rear.[2] Headquarters are here today. The 3rd Division is a league behind us.

Yours &c.
G.H.

---

[1] This incident seems to be fictitious. It was probably an echo of the action at Morales (see note, 3 p. 71).

[2] The British cavalry were only in the French rear in the sense that they were continually moving past the French right flank.

LETTER XIV

Camp near Tamara, 4½ lea[gues] on the
road from Palencia to Burgos.
9th June 1813.

DEAR BROTHERS,

We entered Palencia about 11 o'clock on the morning of the 7th. King Joseph with 15 squadrons of cavalry left it at 7 o'clock the same morning. Some cavalry entered first, then the Light Division followed by the 4th Division. No English troops have ever been here before. The streets were crowded, the shops mostly shut up & the inhabitants seemed to receive us with real demonstrations of joy. Their *vivas* were loud & general, particularly amongst the women, and the men, who seemed possessed of distinct ideas, bowed and said *'viva'*, but half of them remained wrapped up in their cloaks, too stupid to show any symptom of either surprise or pleasure. I was much amused by the nuns in a convent we passed putting out their handkerchiefs through holes in the top of the building & shaking them.

The Household Troops came after the 4th Division viz : the Life Guards & Blues. They paraded the streets such as they did Piccadilly for they went up one, down another, up again, so whether it was a mistake or not I do not know, but this I know, they kept our baggage an hour in the streets & we were waiting for breakfast all the time very impatiently. We encamped that night on the ground. The French left 3 or 4 hours before. Close to the town they left some of their huts made of boughs of trees for which our men were very much obliged to them.

The town of Palencia is beautifully situated on the banks of a river, has a very handsome cathedral nearly equal to the one at Salamanca & has 3 or 4 more churches. The houses are ill-contrived, dark & dirty. The filth is allowed to collect in the streets about an inch deep in the centre & the stirring up which the crowds of men & horses caused an

The Duke of Wellington, painted by P. E. Stroehling
(*National Army Museum*)

Lt-Gen. Baron Charles von Alten, who commanded the Light Division 1812–14; sketch by T. Heaphy (*National Portrait Gallery*)

Lt-Gen. Sir Rowland Hill, sketch by T. Heaphy (*National Portrait Gallery*)

intolerable smell. The town is about the size of Huntingdon, has a mud wall round it & two or three entrances. The only defence was a breastwork made by strong stakes driven into the ground & earth at one gate. You have no idea what a crowd there is when a division, much more of course a corps of three divisions, encamps near a large town. The shops & streets are crowded with officers and soldiers of the 3 nations.

The whole army is, I believe, within a league of this[1] & you will see by the map what a vast tract of country we have passed over in a little time. The weather has been very cool & favourable until yesterday. It rained a little on the march & about 4 o'clock it began raining very hard & continued until 8 o'clock this morning. At night it began to blow exceedingly hard. I was obliged to jump out of bed & hold hard at the pole while the servants drove in the pegs.

We moved here at 6 o'clock, about $\frac{1}{2}$ a league, & are halting how long I do not know. I suppose till the commissaries bring up their stores.

Bread is here cheap. It is a most beautiful country for corn & vines. Wine $2\frac{1}{2}$d per pint. We had showers this morning but it seems clearing up. The ground I am sitting on is as wet as it usually is in England in April. You would feel very much alarmed to be ordered to pitch a tent &, with a thin mattress and two blankets, make yourself comfortable in a meadow after wet days & showery all night, yet this is our case & I assure you I sleep as comfortable as I have done in Wood Street. We have not [been], nor are we likely soon to be, in a house. There is a general shout in the camp every hour caused by a hare being put up &, by the shouting, he generally runs towards the column & is killed, tho' I have seen several pass through & escape. Or you are entertained with the horses or donkeys making love, for the knife is never used in this country. It is all very pleasant while they confine themselves to their comedies in the day-time. In the night it causes great commotion among the tent strings & pegs. Their oratories are very regular. We have 2 or 3 in the day & about 2 in the course of the night. Some well known performer starts in

---

[1] The army on this day was rather closer than it had been on earlier days but not as close as Hennell supposed. The heads of the three Anglo-Portuguese columns covered a front of fifteen miles and the northern (Spanish) column was even further away.

full tone & in half a minute the whole of the donkeys and mules in the division, to the number of 2 or 3 join in the chorus & never cease until they are quite exhausted.

The country where we have just passed through is where the Moors & Spaniards often fought. We passed yesterday one of the spots where one of the most celebrated battles was fought. The country is very level. We passed 2 or 3 leagues which would be taken for a plain but what is called table-land, that is, all the hills about seem as if at a certain height levelled artificially. The town we halted at when I sent off my last letter (Ampudia) is situated on the lower level between two hills. From the edge of one of these you have a prospect of immense extent and may count 50 or 60 towns & villages regularly situated about a league from each other. Scarcely a tree is to be seen for leagues together till you come to a wood. We generally get old vines & timber from old houses for fire-wood.[1] Most of the villages have a Moorish castle & wall round them which are still strong & heavy & nearly all alike . . . built all of stone & are not much destroyed. The inside is divided into different apartments & on the top [are] loopholes for arrows or musquetry.

We are now only 24 leagues, 6 or 7 days march, from the Ebro. If they defend Burgos it will most likely take us 3 weeks or more & to many will be the finish of their journey of life. We are now 10 leagues from it.

Tovar, 13th June, 4 o'clock. We arrived here (a village 5 lea[gues] N. of Burgos). On the 10th we encamped at Lantadilla, a village on the borders of New Castille, on the 11th at Villasandino & on the 12th at Isar, 3 leagues from Burgos, so you see we have been making a circuit rather north. At 12 o'clock on the 12th we heard cannon & understood there had been skirmishing all day. We moved through Isar to a hill 2½ leagues from Burgos. In sight of it the cavalry came up with the French about ½ a league to our right. They formed squares & guns played upon them & drove them over a river but did

---

[1] Wellington issued constant and stringent orders against taking timber from houses for firewood saying, in one of them, 'The Commander of the Forces is ashamed to acknowledge that the British troops have, in many instances, done more mischief to the country in this manner than has been done by the enemy.' He was never able to stop the practice and it is clear from this letter that the officers would not enforce the order since only by taking house timbers could they find the fuel to cook their rations.

not much annoy them.[1] This was a very fatiguing day. We were detained on the road which was very bad & it rained hard all the afternoon. We saw the French retire in haste. Our company was for town duty. I had charge of a guard in the porch of the church. I got my blankets dried & had tea & beef steaks & slept most delightfully. At 8 o'clock next morning moved toward Burgos. As we were waiting for our regiment Lord Wellington & staff came by. Lord [Fitzroy] Somerset said 'Well, did you hear the explosion?' We then learnt that the castle & the whole of the works [of Burgos] were blown up this morning at 6 o'clock – the most convincing proof they could give of their incapacity to stand before us. Lord Wellington came back in half an hour & our column was immediately turned & ordered to move in a northerly direction. It is supposed we are endeavouring to turn their flank & cross the Ebro. Our supplies will come by Santander.[2]

We have not halted a day since we left Salamanca & I suppose are not likely to do so yet. The Hussar Brigade & K.G.L[3] are marching with us. We have been marching today about 3 leagues from Isar in a beautiful valley. The inhabitants came out & the women sang & danced as we passed. I was never in better health in my life though very hungry sitting in a ploughed field writing this letter.

All military persons look upon the destroying [of] Burgos as one of the most important events that has happened in the Peninsula. What could [they] not spare 1 or 2,000 men to annoy us as they

---

[1] On 12 June Wellington detached two brigades of cavalry and the Light Division from the centre column to demonstrate against the flank of the French forces which were trying to make a stand in front of Burgos which was threatened by the right column of the allied army. The French made no stand once they saw the threat to their right and retired, losing fifteen men and a gun which was captured by the Fourteenth Light Dragoons.

[2] Wellington had started to plan the switch of his base from Lisbon to 'one of the ports in the north of Spain' as early as 28 April but in the event the Royal Navy were very slow in making the change and it was two or three months before large quantities of supplies started arriving by the shorter route.

[3] The King's German Legion was recruited into the British service from the remnants of the Hanoverian army. It was the two dragoon regiments of the Legion which had broken the French squares at Garçia Hernandez on 23 July 1812 (see p. 31) and the 1st Hussars, K.G.L. was the cavalry regiment which usually worked with the Light Division. By common consent it was the best cavalry unit in the army.

might have done at Burgos? It would have cost us that number to take it & have detained us 3 weeks or more, though we should have been sure of it & we did not come this time with *one gun*.[1]

YOURS &C.
G.H.

---

[1] It was a common criticism of Wellington's attack on Burgos in 1812 that he had not brought up enough heavy artillery against it. He brought with him only three 18-pounders and two of these were damaged early in the bombardment so that only one could be fired with a full charge.

LETTER XV

DEAR BROTHER,

This is our route since my last. Tovar, 13th June; Quintananiar, 14th; Villalta & Pesada, 15th; Puente Arenas, 16th; Medina [de Pomar], 17th. Espejo we left to our right yesterday. On the 14th we had a long and fatiguing march. My mare had a nail run in her back. Prudence said 'Do not ride!' I was more fatigued than I have been the whole campaign. Owing to our bearing down on Burgos we had to make forced marches & they are very fatiguing. The commissaries cannot get the stores up, so we do not have our rations regular. The last three days we have only had 2 oz. bread, 2 oz flour each man, officers the same.[1] The first two days, viz. 13th & 14th, we were in corn country & by sending forward we could buy some but since that we have been able to get very little and that at 1/- per lb.

On the 16th we had to pass a branch of the Ebro. After marching 2 leagues we had to descend a wall on the edge of it filling it up [sic]. The surface is composed of large & small stones, some fixed, some loose & very irregular. After winding round tremendous perpendicular precipices for $\frac{1}{2}$ a mile we came to a town & saw a most beautiful valley filled with fruit trees, gardens & corn. Cherries were the only fruit ripe. I was too much fatigued to go out of my way to get any. We kept on a mile further and passed the river & encamped on this side. The shallow parts about knee deep, the deepest parts breast high, the stream very rapid. The valley is filled with villages, almost every $\frac{1}{2}$ mile there is one. We procured fine fresh butter here for $\frac{1}{2}$ dollar per lb. & plenty of wine but not good. There were several

---

[1] Each officer and man was entitled to 1 lb of meat, 1 lb of biscuit (or 1$\frac{1}{2}$ lb of bread) and a quart of beer (or a pint of wine or $\frac{1}{4}$ pint of spirits) daily. On this advance the commissariat was not able to keep up with the army but the supply of meat never failed as it travelled with the divisions on the hoof.

fields of garden beans, just ripe, & directly the regiment piled arms they were covered by our locusts. It was near ½ an hour before the general observed it and sounded the *Assembly* & placed a sentry over them, but every havresack was full. We had no bread that day so I was glad to see it.

Genl. Cole (the 4th Division) followed our column & our baggage in his rear. We got in at ½ past 3, the baggage at ½ past 7. When near the enemy or on forced marches we seldom get our baggage before 6 or 7 o'clock so that we throw breakfast, dinner & supper into one meal & have tea, beef steaks and vegetables, if we can get them, and then, after attending to our horses, go to bed.

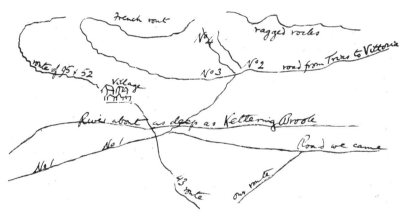

Hennell's sketchmap of the action at San Milan, 18 June 1813

The next day I was for baggage guard. We this day (18th) kept on the side of the river, for a league it runs between two precipices nearly perpendicular, the most beautiful I ever have seen in my life. Every place, except the directly perpendicular rocks, covered with shrubs & trees. The road was horrid. Medina [de Pomar] is on the other side of the other branch of the Ebro. There was sugar & coffee & French brandy to be had at 15d per pint. In the valley we passed the 5th & 1st Divisions. They took a different road from us. Next day (17th) we passed a mountain where the 4th Division bore off to our left. After a march of 3 or 4 leagues over a rocky barren country we encamped. Next day (18th), after marching along a beautiful valley for about 2 leagues, we heard a brisk skirmishing fire in front of us. It was our advanced guard (1st batt. 95th). In a quarter of an hour headquarters passed us. In $\frac{1}{4}$ [hour] more we moved on & filed up a mountain. The left brigade (viz: 52nd, 1st & 3rd *Caçadores* & 3rd Batt. 95th) passed along the valley. We halted at the top in open column. Saw the French for the first time since Burgos. The valley they were passing along as fast as they could go. The 1st batt. 95th extended over their flanks within pistol shot of them, rattling away as fast as they could. About $\frac{1}{2}$ a mile from us (No. 1) we heard they disturbed the village some time. In a $\frac{1}{4}$ of an hour we saw troops coming filing through the pass (No. 2) where only 2 or 3 can pass abreast. We at first thought them Spaniards, but were soon convinced they were French by their running. All of us, both officers and men, cried out 'Why the deuce don't they move us down there upon them?' It was the 2nd brigade of the 35th Division (a light one)[1] & we could not tell how many troops they had to pass. In a little time we saw their baggage coming. Our men became outrageous, swearing they were never employed when there was anything to be got by it. The French were $\frac{1}{2}$ a mile from us at this moment. We saw the *Caçadores* at full run extend & open [fire] upon their baggage at No. 3. Their [the French] commander found the 95th in a village so made for the 1st hill then the second, much higher & behind which were others higher still. In this time the 95th extended & the 52nd behind them in line coming up one hill as they mounted the other. They immediately turned to the mountains of their right in disorder. The 95th immediately opened upon them; the 52nd extended & did so also. During this time they were hurrying the baggage up the hill (No. 4) under a very heavy fire from the *Caçadores*. It kept diminishing as it went & very little got beyond the ragged rocks & what did was taken. They intended to come down the hill, where the 52nd met them, & get on the road. The other brigade was going but, after seeing the 95th, they were completely dismayed & ran in disorder to the mountains.

At this time we were ordered down to the village. Six of our companies were formed near it, two at the pass & two at the colours (I being one of the senior ensigns was with the colours) in the village. In an hour our people began to bring in prisoners and plunder, of

---

[1] The French division was in fact the Fifth Division of the Army of Portugal, commanded by General Anthoine Louis Maucune, and was not 'a light one' indeed, unusually among French divisions it had no light infantry battalions on its strength.

which the *Caçadores* had a rich prize as they took most of the baggage. I am glad they did for they well deserved it. The 1st 95th [&] 52nd took a large quantity. They pursued the enemy a league & a half. They were coming back straggling for two or three hours with prisoners & plunder.[1]

At 5 o'clock we were ordered to advance & support the 5th Division as they were engaged.[2] As soon as Genl. Hill's division came to relieve us, which was at 6 o'clock, we moved on a league & halted half a league from Espejo to which place the rest of the division had moved. Our men took the baggage belonging to the medical officers of the French division. It was large & complete. It was droll to see some of the men return with their plunder. You will see one loaded with bread, another with an officer's coat on, another with a havresack full of bark[3] and there was one with 10 mules.

The French lost in the course of the day 1,000 men. Our loss was 1 officer, 2 sergeants, 20 rank & file killed & wounded.[4] Our officers say they never saw the French behave so ill – they seemed completely panic-struck. I hear several Spanish regiments were despatched after them in the mountains.

Yesterday we started after them at daylight, leaving Espejo on our right. Above the village we found their bivouac, the fires not all out.

---

[1] On 18 June 1813 the Light Division, led by a squadron of the 1st Hussars, K.G.L., surprised the 1st brigade of Maucune's division which was resting in the village of San Milan. While the left brigade of the Light Division was pursuing the broken fugitives of this formation, Maucune's 2nd brigade emerged unexpectedly from a track 'out of an opening between two perpendicular rocks'. They were as surprised as their colleagues but they posed a threat to the rear of the pursuing British brigade and were attacked in their turn by the right brigade (including the Forty Third). The French lost 300 prisoners and all their baggage and King Joseph considered Maucune's division so demoralized that he assigned it to guard the baggage. It was thus not available for the battle of Vitoria three days later.

[2] On the same day as the action at San Milan, the Fifth Division skirmished with the rearguard of the Army of Portugal under General Honoré Reille at Osma, six miles to the north east. The Light Division did not manage to arrive to take part also in this fighting.

[3] Peruvian Bark or Quinine.

[4] The French loss on this day was about 720 in the two actions. The British loss mentioned by Hennell seems to be that of the Light Division. In the two actions the allied army lost 180 killed and wounded.

After passing a mountain & coming into the valley, as we halted we heard a smart fire commence on our left, just over the mountain a mile from us. We were quite as much in advance as the fire, so made no doubt that we should gain the height before them. We saw several on top of a hill. A very brisk fire continued from 12 till 5 o'clock. I have not heard the result.[1]

At 6 o'clock our baggage was ordered up & we encamped & to my surprise we halt today. Our great concern in these forced marches is for our baggage animals. Scarcely a mess are without mules stolen or knocked up, though my two horses are pretty well. All our comforts depend on the baggage animals. I have no idea what this halt is for.

G.H.

---

[1] The firing was caused by the Fourth Division attacking the rearguard of the Army of Portugal on the line of the river Bayas near Subijana de Morillas. Wellington intended the Light Division to fall on the French flank but General Reille retreated too quickly to be caught.

5 Vitoria

The plain of Vitoria into which the French had retreated is an oval of undulating ground about twelve miles long and, at its widest, seven miles across. The river Zadorra enters it through a gap in the surrounding mountains in the north-eastern curve and then turns and flows almost due west for eight miles. There, at the village of Tres Puentes it makes a sharp bend and meanders southward until it leaves the plain through another gap at the western end of the plain with the heights of La Puebla on its eastern bank.

The French were concerned only with fighting a delaying action if they had to fight at all. They devoted their main strength, four divisions, to blocking the approach to Vitoria on the left bank of the river but, having experienced Wellington's recent practice of turning their right, they placed two divisions north of Vitoria where the Bilbao road came through yet another gap in the mountains. Two divisions and King Joseph's Guard were in reserve. The main strength of the French army, was divided into two blocks six miles apart and with their backs to each other.

Wellington's plan for 21 June was a complicated one on exterior lines. He divided his army into four columns each containing two Anglo-Portuguese divisions. Two of these, the right under Hill and the right centre (which included the Light Division) under his own control, were to enter the plain at the southern end with one column on each side of the Zadorra. The left column, commanded by Graham, was to attack due south down the Bilbao road and the left centre column would come over the mountains from the north west. It was obvious that the timing of these four independent attacks would be difficult and in the event Graham's column was late arriving and met stiff opposition. Nevertheless, thanks largely to the mistakes of the French command, the other three columns were wholly successful and by nightfall the French were streaming away in disorder towards Pamplona on a secondary road. They had lost more than 8,000 men (of whom 2,000 were prisoners) while the attackers had lost only 5,000. King Joseph made no further attempt to make a stand until the army was safely in France.

General Clausel, with 10,000 men of the Armies of the North and of Portugal, had been trying to join the king but failed to discover his whereabouts and his advancing cavalry came within sight of the battlefield twenty-four hours after the battle ended. Wellington made a spirited but belated attempt to cut him off from France, which resulted in a week's hard but abortive marching for the Light Division; but by the end of the first week of July the army had settled down along the Franco-Spanish frontier to cover the investments of Pamplona and San Sebastian, the only remnants except Santoña of the Bonaparte kingdom of Spain.

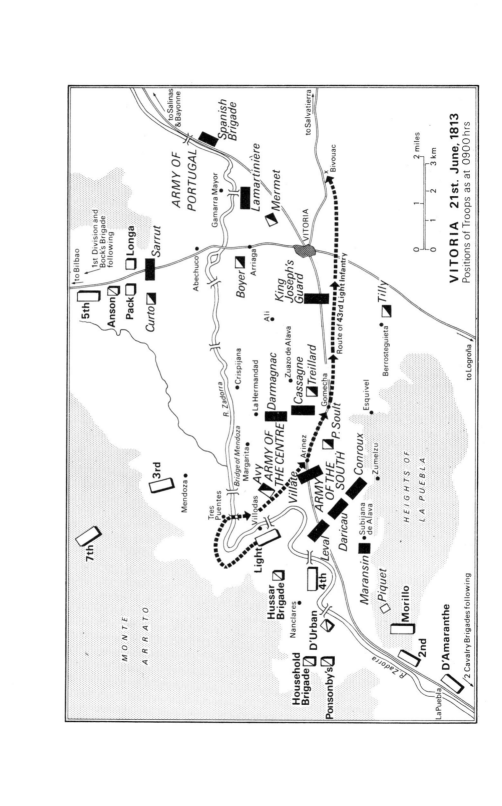

VITORIA 21st. June, 1813
Positions of Troops as at 0900 hrs

to Salinas & Bayonne
to Salvatierra
Spanish Brigade
ARMY OF PORTUGAL
Gamarra Mayor
Lamartinière
Mermet
to Bilbao
1st Division and Bock's Brigade following
Longa
Sarrut
5th
Anson
Pack
Curto
Abechuco
Arriaga
Boyer
King Joseph's Guard
VITORIA
Bivouac
Route of 43rd Light Infantry
Ali
Tilly
R. Zadorra
Crispijana
La Hermandad
Zuazo de Alava
Darmagnac
Cassagne
Treillard
Gomecha
Berrostegueta
to Logroña
Bridge of Mendoza
Margarita
Avy
ARMY OF THE CENTRE
Arinez
Villatte
ARMY OF THE SOUTH
P. Soult
Esquivel
Tres Puentes
Villodas
Conroux
Zumelzu
3rd
Mendoza
Leval
Daricau
Subijana de Alava
MONTE ARRATO
7th
Light
4th
Maransin
Piquet
Morillo
HEIGHTS OF LA PUEBLA
Hussar Brigade
D'Urban
Nanclares
Household Brigade
Ponsonby's
D'Amaranthe
2nd
R. Zadorra
2 Cavalry Brigades following
La Puebla

0   1   2 miles
0   1   2   3 km

LETTER XVI

Camp on the banks of the river Aragon, near Caseda,
2 lea[gues] S. of Sanguessa.
June 29th 1813.

DEAR BROTHERS,

This is the first hour I have had to write since my last of the 20th inst. We halt today. One reason is [that] if we did march we should leave half behind us – they are completely knocked up. Every hour since my last is so full of incident that I shall give you it as much at length as I can.

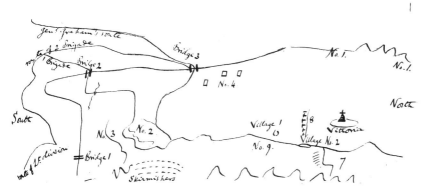

Hennell's sketchmap of the Battle of Vitoria, 21 June 1813

On the 21st our own division marched. I was in orders for the charge of the baggage which was to march at 7 o'clock. We did so & went round that mountain from which we had heard firing the night before. After marching ½ a league the baggage halted for the reserve artillery & Household troops to pass. We then mov'd up the hill & I there learned that a general engagement was begun. I gave the sergeant charge of the baggage & immediately galloped on & at the top of the hill saw the whole of the French army in a plain with

[87]

Vitoria in their rear & a smart skirmish on my right. Ours was the first brigade.

On arriving I found the 43rd in front & came up to them as it was going round a hill to a wood on the top, the river running just below. We remained there about an hour & then marched round by No. 2 bridge which was *not* defended, to a hill overlooking the whole plain with a wall in front breast high & we formed behind it. They gave us a salute with one or two guns from bridge No. 3 which did no damage. This was to begin with.

I have called this spot a plain because it is so in comparison with this mountainous country surrounding. It is an oval form (No. 1) but it is crowded with little hills 3 or 400 yards asunder, very disadvantageous for a retiring army. The hill (No. 2) in front was the highest. No. 3 was a line of artillery and infantry well formed to defend bridge No. 1.

The 2nd Division began the battle on our right. In the meantime our main force, viz: 1st, 7th, 3rd & 4th divisions moved round to their right.[1] We had between 70 & 80,000 men: French 60,000.[2] We all expected they would have defended the bridges obstinately and their positions more so, but they most shamefully and very unlike Frenchmen gave up both with scarcely a shadow of defence.

About 10 o'clock the 1st 95th moved along the river side, the 2nd brigade moving round to attack bridge No. 3. The river is fordable in some parts. The bridge was lined with skirmishers, 2 or 3 troops of cavalry & 2 guns. The 2nd brigade sent skirmishers below the bridge. They opened a fire just as Graham's columns[3] came in sight. At a distance of $\frac{1}{4}$ a mile the 95th was running down to flank them [the French]. They had a large body in squares (No. 4). All now

---

[1] The Fourth Division was not on the left but immediately on the right of the Light Division. This must be a slip of the pen since later in the letter Hennell refers to the Fourth being on the right.

[2] Wellington, who had left one Anglo-Portuguese division near the Ebro to guard his communications and had detached a Spanish force towards Bilbao, had 72,000 men (of whom 11,000 were Spaniards) at Vitoria. The French army had about 58,000.

[3] Graham's column was more than six miles away marching south down the Bilbao road and had not yet come into action. The troops who appeared on the left of the Light Division were Picton's Third Division leading Dalhousie's left centre column.

began to return to them as fast as they could run. We then moved down the hill in open column of companies and, at No. 5, formed line and, with a few skirmishers in front, were ordered to attack the hill. A sergeant was in the centre with [one] Colour and myself with the other. We were to make for the centre of the middle & highest hill, the 17th Portuguese supporting us. When we were ½ way up the hill, they [the French] disappeared without firing a shot.[1] During this time the 2nd brigade were moving round the hill and our columns were crossing the river. Their [French] line (No. 2) moved off before them. We moved round the hill & heard a heavy fire on our left & very near. We moved on to a hill 300 yards farther & there the cannon balls began to hiss over our heads. We mov'd on to a hill 100 yards from the village, No. 1, a very heavy fire continuing on our left. We formed line about 20 yards from the bank (2 yds high). Here we had a very strong fire from a battery of theirs, No. 6, of balls & shells, while the 95th & some other troops were attacking the village which they defended well.

The first ball that came was a spent one. It struck the ground about 50 yards from us & was coming straight for me but it rebounded about 10 yards [from me] & went to my left, just over the heads of the men & struck our old colonel [Daniel Hearn] on the arm. He called out but was not much hurt as it came about as swift as a swallow flies.[2] Finding the fire heavy, we moved under a bank & lay down. At that moment a shell came gently hopping direct for me but it was polite enough to halt on top of the bank about 6 yards from us.

---

[1] The immediate French guard on the river by the bridge of Tres Puentes was a weak dragoon brigade (474 sabres). They were supported by an infantry division, the 'large body in squares', near Ariñez. The reason why 'they disappeared without firing a shot' was that Jourdan announced 'loudly and publicly that all the movements on our right [i.e. the attacks around Tres Puentes] were feints to which no attention must be paid, and that if [the French] lost the battle it would be because the mountains on the left of the Zadorra remained in enemy hands'. He, therefore, sent the division to counter attack Hill's column on the heights of La Puebla. He should have had two more reserve divisions but these he had sent to counter a wholly imaginary threat from due south of Vitoria.

[2] It can scarcely have been a cannon ball which struck Lieutenant Colonel Hearn since he was not returned as wounded and even the smallest cannon ball travelling 'as swift as a swallow flies' would have smashed his arm. It can only have been a spent musket ball.

We lay down & in about 1 minute it burst doing no harm.[1] In another minute a ball struck the close column of the 17th Portuguese not a yard from the place the 43rd colours had just left & about 16 yards from us. It killed a sergeant & took off the leg of each of the ensigns with the colours. This was about 2 o'clock.

We halted there a $\frac{1}{4}$ of an hour until the village was taken by the 95th, who captured their cannon.[2] We then moved in open column to our right, the battery, No. 6, firing as fast as possible all the time. During this time some Spanish troops were skirmishing with a flock (for they were all scattered) of French on the side of the mountain[3] and a body of French between us & them, which the 4th Division was chasing, kept retiring and taking up good positions & most cowardly abandoning them till we came to the village, No. 2. This is to be said for them that their principal force was on our left & was retiring hotly engaged. The 3rd Division had most of it (the attack) & were nearly a mile before them so that they were afraid of being cut off. At the same time they had to support their skirmishers on the mountain as they were more behind still. We were about even [i.e. level] with them & against village No. 2, on the right of which there was a wood. We moved to our right hoping to cut them off but they ran too fast for us.

Just after we came out of the wood we found a little valley & they had regularly taken up an excellent position. We formed line on the hill while the one opposite us was taken. The 45th was in line in the

---

[1] Fuses, and especially French fuses, were very unreliable. George Napier told of a man in the Fifty Second, 'an Irishman and an old marine, a most worthless drunken dog, [who] ran up to a thirteen inch shell, the fuze of which was still burning, and striking it with his spade, knocked it out. Taking the immense shell in his hands he came and presented it to me, saying, 'There she is for you now, your honour. By Jasus, she'll do you no harm since I knocked the life out of the cratur!'

[2] This was the village of Ariñez which, with three guns, was captured by two companies of the Rifles but lost to an immediate counter-attack. It was recaptured by the rest of 1st battalion Ninety Fifth with Wellington riding in their midst, and supported by the Connaught Rangers.

[3] These Spaniards belonged to Pablo Morillo's division, attached to Hill's column. In fact they had heavy fighting, losing some 300 men. On top of the heights, invisible to Hennell, was a brigade of Second Division and it was this fighting on the heights that was so successful in keeping Jourdan's attention focused on his left, thus leaving his centre weakly defended.

Lt-Gen. Sir William Beresford, Marshal of the Portuguese
Army, by R. Rothwell (*National Portrait Gallery*)

Marshal Marmont, Duke of Ragusa; engraving by J. N. Joly after Meyer (*British Museum*)

Marshal Soult, Duke of Dalmatia; engraving after Henri Grévedon (*Musée de l'Armée, Paris*)

hollow ready to charge up the hill, No. 8, more in the rear, on which were 18 or 20 pieces of cannon playing upon our regiment & [village No.] 2. They were ½ a mile distant. We kept driving in their skirmishers to a line formed on a hill to our right, No. 7. (No. 8 their cannon; No. 9 our line). After this a Portuguese regiment moved round their left &, appearing on their flank, they all set off from that, & the next, No. 9, leaving all their artillery.[1]

(*Note*. The French had no idea of our attacking them today. If we had done so they would have had batteries all along the hill, & if they had been obliged to retire, would have returned to this position & suddenly opened upon us a most destructive fire. It was their intention to attack us, but Lord Wellington had a better head than any of their miserable generals who commanded them on that day.)[2]

All this time Genl. Graham was pressing their main force on the[ir] right. It was near here that two of our officers [Major John Duffy & Lieutenant George Houlton] were wounded. They did not maintain their position more than ½ an hour. Several of our officers remarked, & I think it just, that cannon make more noise and alarm than they do mischief. Many shots were fired at us but we suffered little from them. A young soldier is much more alarmed at a nine pounder shot passing within 4 yds. of his head than he is of a bullet at a distance of as many inches, although one would settle him as effectively as the

---

[1] The French had 76 pieces of artillery on this position which stretched from Crispijana, near the river to Esquival on the slopes of the heights. Not all these guns were captured here, some got away to become entangled in the chaos in and around Vitoria. The reason why the French kept taking up and then abandoning good positions was a failure in command. Gazan, commanding on the French left, was ordered to fall back to a position which Jourdan would point out to him and retreated capably enough by a succession of brigades, taking up delaying positions. Unfortunately Jourdan never gave him the promised order to stop and, being a literally minded officer, Gazan continued his retreat, thus exposing the flank of the divisions on his right which were forced to conform to his withdrawal.

[2] The French had no intention of attacking. They had halted at Vitoria to give their baggage train time to get closer to France. They did not expect Wellington to attack them there because they had become conditioned to his repeated turning movements on their right and expected him to turn them again on 21 June. On the morning of the battle Joseph and Jourdan had decided to pull back to the Crispijana–Esquival line so as to have their men more concentrated but Wellington attacked them before they had time to give the orders.

other. Artillery makes great havoc when in close column. The French are very correct in aiming their artillery. [At] ½ past 3, in passing the line the 45th occupied in the valley, I saw 10 or 12 killed or wounded in the space of as many yards owing to the fire kept up on them from the hill.

Upon their cannons ceasing to fire, our guns galloped after them as fast as they could move. They began to run faster than we could follow. We chased them by Vitoria in grand style, leaving them no time to save their immense baggage. They took up a position 1½ miles beyond Vitoria which they abandoned as soon as some 9 pounders from a hill close to Vitoria played upon them. As they went up the hill in the greatest disorder, scattering like a flock of sheep, we kept moving forward leaving Vitoria ½ a mile to our right. After this the Household troops, viz : the [Life] Guards & Blues, came galloping by us. I do not know what good they did, if any I am sure you would hear of it.

At 6 o'clock we came up to a village where were 8 or 10 wagons overturned with all kinds of valuable baggage attended by dragoons, Spaniards & stragglers plundering them.[1] The smell of French brandy was very strong, I am sorry I cannot tell the taste. The soldiers were not allowed to touch a drop. If they attempted it the officers knocked it out of their hands. However, as they had to march over a great quantity it could not be entirely prevented. We saw the French no more this day. We continued marching till dark, 9 o'clock, passing more wagons overturned & baggage of every description, including flocks of sheep, goats, bullocks, asses, mules, horses &c.

---

[1] John Cooke also described this scene. 'The road to Pamplona was choked with carriages filled with imploring ladies, waggons loaded with specie, powder and ball, wounded soldiers intermixed with droves of oxen, sheep, goats, mules, asses, milch cows, *filles de chambres* and officers. In fact such a jumble surely was never seen before. Our brigade marched past this strange scene of domestic strife in close column, nor did I see a soldier attempt to quit the ranks.' Other brigades were not so scrupulous, nor were the stragglers of both armies and the camp followers. Wellington was justifiably angry and wrote 'The soldiers of the army have got among them about a million sterling, with the exception of about 100,000 dollars which were got for the military chest. The night of the battle, instead of being passed in getting rest and food for the pursuit of the following day were passed by the soldiers in looking for plunder. The consequence was that they were incapable of marching and were totally knocked up.'

At last we halted at the side of a narrow lane stopped up with wagons, our artillery in front of us firing as long as they could see. We here found a flock of sheep, mostly killed & tumbled one upon another into a deep ditch. In the same ditch were 2 or 3 pieces of cannon, overturned, horses & mules with them. You can hardly form any conception of the scene here – everyone busy & most employed in getting the sheep out of the ditch, while others were skinning them, the whole, as you may suppose, knocked up. In the morning I was fortunate in being on the baggage so [had] had an excellent breakfast & took the precaution to put some bread & meat in my pocket. Many of the officers had nothing all day. From bridge No. 1 to Vitoria is 2 leagues & we marched 1½ leagues beyond it. The division then formed upon a hill close by. The baggage, of course, could not get up.

I shall now conclude this with a short description of the scene presented on halting. The wood of the wagons supplied fuel & about every 2 yds. square was a fire & a circle round it. One will describe the whole – one making dough boys (flour & water mixed) swearing all the time at one for not producing a frying pan, at another for getting in his light; another giving a young soldier a thump for crossing between him & the fire while he plastered his blistered feet. The poor creature is turning round to beg his pardon, when he treads upon another, who threatens to upset him if he does not sit down. A woman who is undressing by his side (perhaps the wife of one of the party) raises her shrill voice & blasts him for not being quick. An old soldier sits smoking his pipe & frying the mutton or skimming the pot, while a dirty fist seizes the mutton, and another equally so lays hold of it & it is torn asunder by a knife with edge & back alike. The whole is shortly devoured & they lie down to sleep in their blankets. It was a cloudy but fine day. I had not the slightest touch of shot or shell.

YOURS &c.
G.H.

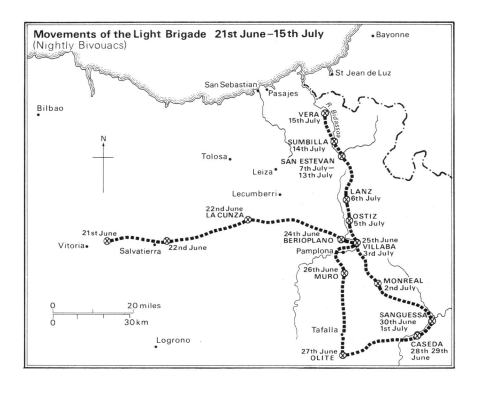

LETTER XVII

6th July 1813.
Camp near Lanz, 4 lea[gues] from Pamplona,
9 lea. from 1st town in France & 11 lea.
from Bayonne.

DEAR BROTHERS,

The victory of the 21st June was, I believe, as complete a victory as we have gained in the Peninsula & attended with great advantages. We have driven the main French army out of Spain.

I shall now give you some details of their retreat & you will see how delightfully wet, hungry & cold we have been in following up this victory. Officers are not allowed to plunder, or men either. If it was allowed you would not have three men to follow up an enemy in one league. All things taken are sold & equally distributed. After halting, several of us found a gun with 8 horses & mules thrown into a deep ditch. After much fatigue we succeeded in getting them out and I got an amazing large mule as large as most English horses & worth 200 dollars, which to my great regret I was obliged to give up with all the rest, next morning to be sold by auction for the benefit of the division. One officer of the 95th took a gun & 6 horse with 3 men so I cannot consider mine a hard case.

Next morning at 10 o'clock we marched 3 leagues to the end of a plain & to the entrance of a defile between very high mountains, a river between & halted in a beautiful wood at sun set. It there began to rain & blow & was as cold as England in November. It rained all night & wetted us through. At daylight marched. If it had been fine the road would have been bad but as it was it was almost impassable. The road was 2 yards wide with large & small loose stones & mud & water well mixed up by French feet & prevented from settling by the English. Our division was in front with a few cavalry & some guns. We soon met parties of 3, 4, 6, 10 & 12 prisoners hobbling back quite

[95]

dejected at being taken so near France. This day's march was quite as bad as any in the retreat last July [November?]. We marched, or rather crawled, 3 leagues by 2 o'clock rain continuing all the time & passed through Salvatierra. King Joe slept here last night. The inhabitants told us that the French who were passing all the morning were completely tired & dejected. Their camps were always close to a village which is completely ransacked. On their approach the inhabitants always left & carried what they could into the mountains. Every door that could had been wrenched off for a shed, and the furniture used for firing. We passed a fine village in flames & some of the roofs falling in. It had now rained tremendously & our regiments were allowed to go into the houses not on fire, which were quite stripped. After making a fire & getting dry at ½ past 5, 6 o'clock we were ordered to fall in, rain continuing, & moved to the next village, a mile further, with full expectation of quartering as it was uncertain whether the baggage containing the tents &c. would get up. The French were passing a village half a league in front of us with our guns playing on them.

As we were coming into the town, I was cheering myself with the expectation of a good fire in a house but the Quartermaster General at this moment passed & ordered us to encamp, which did not raise my spirits to a very high pitch. We then moved with melancholy looks to a wood ½ a mile off & I there sat down under a tree, rain continuing [at] 7 o'clock. In half an hour the joyful news of 'fall in' arrived (this order is seldom considered so) & we returned to the village. In ½ an hour I was in a kitchen with a large fire but had a violent headache.

We marched the next day (24th) at daybreak. Heavy showers all day, the roads as bad or worse & passing prisoners as before. About 12 o'clock they opened on our advanced guard all the artillery we had left them, which was one 9-pounder and one howitzer in a village on the main road to Pamplona. They detained us very little time. The French general's lady was overturned here & taken. We passed on the road 4 men killed & wounded by the same ball; they lay in the space of 2 yards. One was shot through the lower part of his body, another both thighs broke, a third his legs & a fourth his ankles. These were quite sensible. One said 'Pray kill me' & another asked for some water. I had nothing to give them. One of our men, more feeling than the rest, said 'Poor fellow, if I had some, I would give it you.' Here we took their 9-pounder & howitzer so that they marched into Pamplona without artillery and, I believe, baggage.[1]

We halted at a village $1\frac{3}{4}$ leagues from Pamplona. As my dinner was getting ready my *patron* & *patrona* (a man & woman of the house) came in from the mountains. She was pale & fatigued & stood still on entering, exclaiming at every look 'Oh Jesus!' Everything was broken. The man had been pursued by a French dragoon & had his coat cut & he detained me $\frac{1}{2}$ an hour telling me about it while I was bothering him for bread. He at last went & pulled a loaf from under some sticks in the garden & gave me half. Here they talk half French, half Spanish. The Biscayans have a language of their own.

Strange to say, this night I had no signs of fever & little cold. Next morning I was quite well. Prudence was honouring a bill I drew upon her. Had I been in the habit, as most of our officers are, of getting drunk when they procure good wine, I should in all probability like them have been suffering from ague & fever.

We marched next day (25th) $\frac{1}{2}$ a league & waited for the 4th

---

[1] Having lost 151 guns at Vitoria the French army was left with only one gun and one howitzer. The allied advance guard now consisted of the Light Division, the German Hussars and Ross's troop (the Chestnut), Royal Horse Artillery. They came up with the French rear near Berrioplano, a few miles short of Pamplona. According to George Simmons of the Rifles, 'The only gun the enemy had brought from Vitoria was now turned upon us. The enemy, formed up across the road, gave us a few discharges of grape and round shot. Some Riflemen were ordered to move quickly upon the flank and attack it, the horse artillery giving the enemy a few rounds of shot and shrapnel from two guns. The hussars dashed forward. Poor *Johnny* [the French] in a hurry to get away overturned gun, horses and all. The road had been raised 15 feet over a flat. The side was built up like a wall. It was just the worst place for miles that the animals and gun could have been trundled over.' (*A British Rifleman*: George Simmons, Ed: W. Verner (1899).) There is some doubt about whether the howitzer was also taken. Simmons does not mention it and Hew Ross of the Horse Artillery says in his diary only 'Take an 8-pr., disabling it with our fire.' In a letter written that day he wrote 'today we have taken the only two [pieces] they had remaining'. Wellington's despatch said that the advance guard 'took from them the remaining gun they had. They have entered Pamplona with one howitzer only.'

No other authority mentions 'the French general's lady' being taken on this day. This probably refers to Madame Gazan who was taken trying to get clear of Vitoria on 21 June. She was duly returned to her husband in her own carriage as soon as the road was clear.

Division on a hill within sight of Pamplona, which is situated in a plain with immense mountains surrounding it but too distant to be made use of in attacking the town. From this hill we had a beautiful view of the town. I hear it esteemed as one of the strongest places in Europe but it does not appear anything like so strong as Badajoz. I hear there are only 3,000 men left to defend it. There ought to be at least 10,000. It is supposed that it contains immense property as they have had no time to get it off.[1]

The town was perfectly still & we moved round it to Villava, a very good town, the houses all good. The one I was in held our company, 60 strong, & would have held another. Every chest & drawers was broken open [by the French] & the clothes they did not choose to take away strewed knee-deep on the floor. They demanded of the richest man in the town (a priest) all his shirts, and they even stripped him of his boots. He gave them some excellent wine & because he neither would nor could give them more they cut out his tongue & stabbed him. Some of our officers saw him dead.

I now thought all fatigues over & as I lay in bed, resolving after breakfast to write, the sergeant major entered with orders for a mounted officer to wait upon the Adjutant General for instructions. Ensign Hennell for the above duty. It was to go back with an officer of the 95th to the village we left the night before, wait for the 3rd Division. On the 95th officer's arrival the division was to march on the road to Tafalla. I met it half way on my return.

We immediately heard the object of this march was to intercept Genl. Clausel with between 10 & 15,000 men who could get no intelligence of King Joe. He [Clausel] was within 2 leagues of Vitoria

---

[1] Pamplona had a garrison of 3,600 men and rations for three months. There is no evidence that the place contained 'immense property which they have not been able to get off'. Most of the loot which the French had acquired during their occupation of Spain (except Soult's magnificent collection of Murillos which he had already removed) was recaptured at Vitoria. The governor of Pamplona refused to allow any of the troops from Vitoria to enter the city lest they demoralize his garrison and eat their rations. He made an exception only for King Joseph and his personal staff. Pamplona was not a very strong fortress although its situation, protected on one side by the river Arga, would have made it difficult to the attack. The governor reported that up to 18 June its defences were little more than protection against a surprise attack. In the event it was not besieged but only blockaded. Starvation forced it to surrender on 30 October.

after the battle when the 7th [6th] division turned and chased him. We were to have surprised him &, as the 3rd & 4th Divisions were in our rear would, of course, take all, but an Alcade gave him intelligence & he made off to Tudela, from thence to join Suchet.[1] He caused us a week of hard marching for no good. We then came back after going by Tafalla, Olite, round by Gallipenza, Caseda, Sanguessa, Monreale, Villava & a league further. Mina attacked Clausel in Tudela & made them throw all his cannon in the river. Mina has always had possession of the country about Sanguessa & in Biscay. He will not allow a grain of intelligence to go to or from Clausel. The 6th Division, I hear, is after him [Clausel] with some of the best Spanish troops in the service.[2]

Pamplona is closely invested by Spaniards. The day before yesterday they made redoubts on the hills round it. They fired a shell or two at the working party every half hour. I hear our outposts are in France. Genl. Graham must be very near.[3]

> Yours &c.
> G.H.

---

[1] General Clausel with four divisions, some 10,000 men, had been trying to join King Joseph but had underestimated the speed of his retreat. He heard of the disaster at Vitoria while at Trevino on 22 June and sent patrols to the hills south of the city. Seeing that the British were there in strength, he tried to join the king but when he had collected the garrison of Logroño he heard that the side road he had hoped to take was blocked by a Spanish force. Realizing that Wellington might try to trap him he crossed to the south bank of the Ebro and marched as fast as possible to Saragossa. Wellington heard rather late of his move to Logroño and, as it happened, there was never any real chance of cutting him off. Marshal Suchet commanded the French armies in east Spain, in whose territory Saragossa lay.

[2] Mina y Epoz, the most famous of the Spanish guerrilla leaders, was at about this time made a brigadier in the regular army. During the winter of 1812–13 he had even collected custom duty on French imports into Spain along the western end of the Pyrenees. He did not manage to intercept Clausel on this occasion being able only to harass his rear with some cavalry. The Sixth Division did not continue its pursuit of Clausel but marched instead to the investment of Pamplona.

[3] i.e., near to France. Thomas Graham was commanding the left wing of the army and had closed up to the Bidassoa, the river which marks the Franco-Spanish frontier near the sea.

LETTER XVIII

[San Estevan]
4½ lea[gues] from France. 7½ from Bayonne.
8th July 1813.

DEAR BROTHERS,

On the 26th June we marched 3 leagues on the road to Tafalla, very little rain all day. 27th we had a very long march. The country is mountainous but very fruitful. There is a valley with a walled orchard, about a furlong wide & ½ a mile long, filled with fruit trees. Cherries, plums & apples were selling all along the road and at the end of it is the city of Tafalla, which is the beginning of a level country. Tafalla is a good town & in it are many priests. We passed through it with the Household Troops on our flank. Bands playing, we were well received – huzzas were loud & general. Next day was fine. We passed by Olite & bore 2 leagues to our left, marching for two leagues over very fertile ground covered with most beautiful corn & then 2 leagues farther over a barren country. It was exceedingly hot & the sudden transitions from cold & wet to heat made us feel it doubly.

We halted in a wood for two hours. The baggage came in soon after the columns. There is only one batman allowed to march with the subalterns of a company's baggage. Mine stopped in a village to have the other subaltern's mule shod & detained mine. I went & brought it on myself just in time to start again (4 o'clock). I had just time to get a cup of tea & some bread & butter & to put half a loaf in a havresack & some wine in my canteen. It was said we had 2 leagues farther over mountains. We marched a league over mountains where it might be said there was no road as only one man could pass at a time. Our division, 5,000 strong 3 abreast, occupy a mile in length on a march.

We marched along the rugged banks of the river Aragon, which is very rapid & deep, at a very slow pace. As it became dark the road grew worse. We prowled another hour when we found a check which detained us on the bank another ¾ of an hour. You will see in the map two bridges, one at Caseda & one at a village before it. We now had to lead our horses over rocks we could scarcely pass ourselves. After slipping at every step the horse had frequently a slanting rock sideways & as steep as any part of Greenwich hill, & 1, 2 & sometimes 3 yards to go & then it broke off abruptly & he had $\frac{1}{2}$ a yard to slip down. We moved in this style about $\frac{1}{2}$ an hour till we found we had lost the road when the Brigade Major called out to the company in advance to send back a man to show us the road. They answered that not a man would come back & when he began to scold he got no reply.

The 1st village was just above us on top of the hill. We crawled up & down the hill again & in about $\frac{1}{2}$ an hour crossed the river till we arrived at the camp near Caseda. We immediately fastened our horses to a bayonet [stuck in the ground as a picket] & rolled ourselves up in the blankets off the horses' backs & laid our heads on the saddles. We now only wanted rain to make the night complete. [At] 11 o'clock we were not disappointed in this for in less than $\frac{1}{2}$ of an hour a violent thunder storm came on accompanied with rain which lasted until day light. Notwithstanding this I slept 2 or 3 hours & had the satisfaction of finding myself (on awakening) in the midst of a puddle.

We halted that day as we had not more than $\frac{1}{2}$ the regiment with us & no baggage. The men were coming in all day. The baggage arrived at daylight. The animals taken in action were sold here by auction. My mule sold for 165 dollars.

Next day (30th June) we marched to Sanguessa. The guerrillas have always had possession of the country about here. Mina frequently had his headquarters here. Sanguessa is about the size of Tafalla, a much worse town thickly inhabited & very filthy. After halting a day we marched to Monreale, $4\frac{1}{2}$ leagues. I was in a house but had so many fleas who seemed to enjoy the change of diet from Spanish to English blood that they allowed me little rest.[1]

---

[1] It is surprising that this is the first time that Hennell complains of fleas, which were a constant hazard in both Portugal and Spain. As early as November 1808 William Booth, then in the Ninety Fifth, wrote home that 'If you go into any house you stand a chance of coming out lousy and flea-bitten.' John Burgoyne of the Engineers attributed the trouble to the 'great wooden bedsteads, with ornamental bedheads, which are very alarming as usually producing more bedfellows than one would wish'. Edward Fitzgerald, Tenth Hussars, complained in 1813 that 'The house I am billeted in is swarming with bugs and fleas. They made the most *terrible example* of me so that I am spotted like a *trout.*'

3rd July. Marched at daylight a league on the road we came [on] &, after lying in the field two hours, encamped a mile from Pamplona expecting we were going into the trenches, which is not the pleasantest work we do.

4th July. Halted & working parties were ordered to make redoubts round the town which settled it was to be most strictly invested. On the 5th we took the road to Bayonne & had a beautiful encampment [at Ostiz].

6th. Marched two leagues along the river side & had an encampment exceeding the last in beauty. The hills around, which are part of the Pyrenees, are very high & steep & covered with corn, trees, herbage, heaths & breaks. Yesterday morning we marched over tremendous mountains [the Col de Velate]. The scenery was surprisingly beautiful.

I have brought up my arrear of narrative. Now for a few remarks. You will see by my preceding letter that I might have been absent from the battle of the 21st [Vitoria] as I was on command, yet such is the high sense of honour in our regiment that in all probability they would have joked me about it for some time though this was not my reason for going forward. It was likely to be a general engagement &, supposing it the last we should have, I did not chuse to be absent. A fit of passion is no trial of a man's courage but a whole day's battle really is. If, after 3 or 4 hours fatigue & witnessing the destructive effects of cannon & musketry, you are ordered to charge an enemy you will discover what quantity of that necessary ingredient you possess. There are few but feel something more than usual on going into battle. The 1st is, no doubt, the worst but do not imagine that after the 2nd or 3rd all feeling is lost. Old soldiers know well what a ball can do & many feel more than they express, though I believe we shall not be charged with being unfaithful. Many of our officers said, when we expected to have to force the 1st bridge, 'I do not like the idea of forcing the bridge. How the grape will rattle round us!'

After viewing the enemy you feel at the word 'Fall in' [more] than you do when the 1st ball passes & less as they increase. If you were to come up with us when halted before a general engagement you would not suspect what we were going about. More jokes pass then than at a halt on a wet day & when they move forward every officer is more on the alert than usual. The men wipe out their pans & see that the flint & steel are right as cooly as you would go shooting sparrows.

It is conjectured we shall have a month's pay as a compensation for our plunder. A great deal of it will never see the light, except in England. Commissaries & their clerks have smuggled fine sums. It is reported two were moving back to headquarters to be disposed of by Lord Wellington. I hear Lord Wellington is in a tremendous rage with the cavalry who behaved very bad with respect to plunder. He saw some of the 18th Hussars himself plundering instead of pushing the enemy.[1] The Household Troops were too late to do much good. I hear he expected to do much more than he has,[2] so perhaps his lordship is not so happy as Ensign Hennell, who has gained little & has both his horses with sore backs.

I do not suppose there was ever a person in the army more quizzed than I have been. The officers of the army are none of them half characters. They do not content themselves with a little swearing & joking about serious things but they are generally openly profane & cooly & deliberately take the seat of the scorner. My Bible has been attacked in every way & the more impious the quotation the louder the laugh. Indeed such a pitch has it arrived that what would shock you would not raise a laugh here. I was in company last night with a very intelligent priest who says the French were completely dejected in passing through, some of them crying. He gave us much information of the Biscayans. The language of them [Basque] is

---

[1] Wellington was very angry with the Eighteenth Hussars, writing to London that they 'are a disgrace to the name of a soldier, in action as well as elsewhere; and I propose to draft their horses from them, and to send the men to England, if I cannot get the better of them in any other manner' (29 June). London replied that the regiment 'left England with a very indifferent reputation for discipline' and, in an attempt to improve them, three new troop commanders were introduced to fill death vacancies. In January 1814 Wellington thought them the 'worst commanded and worst officered regiment I have ever met with'.

[2] If Wellington's plan for Vitoria had worked perfectly he might have surrounded the whole French army but, being a realist, he would not have expected everything to succeed in a complicated manoeuvre. There is no evidence that he was less than satisfied with the overwhelming victory he obtained. His aim was to drive the French out of Spain and he succeeded at very moderate cost.

particular & not resembling any other. It is the most expressive language on earth. He says the French can never remain long in Spain. Their manners are so dissimilar to those of the inhabitants.

Yours &c.
G.H.

6 The Pyrenees

An allied invasion of France was the logical consequence of the victory at Vitoria but Wellington was not prepared to undertake such a move while the fortresses of San Sebastian and Pamplona obstructed his sea and land communications. Until they could be reduced he was faced with having to defend a front more than forty miles long and split by the Sierra de Aralar which joins the Pyrenees to the Cantabrian mountains of northern Spain. The Sierra was crossed by few roads, some of them bad and the rest little more than tracks. Cavalry was useless in this terrain and he had only 62,000 infantry and artillery to cover his front on which the French could choose their point of attack. Whenever they did advance it was clearly going to be very difficult to concentrate enough troops to contain them.

The news of Vitoria had reached Napoleon at Dresden on 1 July and he reacted by ordering King Joseph into house arrest and sending Soult to command all the armies 'in Spain and in the Pyrenees'. His orders were to relieve San Sebastian and Pamplona and 'to re-establish my business in Spain'. The marshal found 79,000 men in his field army and, within a fortnight of his return to the army, launched 53,000 of them in two columns aiming for Pamplona. Both columns, despite great numerical superiority, had difficulty in forcing their way through the frontier passes but the eastern column almost reached Pamplona while the western force blocked the best of the passes over the Sierra de Aralar, thus greatly adding to Wellington's difficulties in concentrating to his right in front of Pamplona.

Despite these difficulties there were sufficient allied troops on Sorauren ridge by 28 July to bring Soult's advance to a halt in a battle that caused Wellington to remark: 'I never saw such fighting . . . The battle was fair bludgeon work.' Two days later, as Soult was trying to withdraw, the allies counter-attacked and drove the French back over the frontier with the loss of 13,000. By 2 August the rival armies were back in their original positions.

The Light Division's part in this week of fighting was limited, except for the last two days, to heavy marches over rugged country. They first marched south over the mountains to block the road from Pamplona to San Sebastian and then, when the news of Sorauren reached them, they hastily retraced their steps to harry the French rearguard on the last stages of their retreat.

LETTER XIX

Camp 1 mile from Vera, 1 league from frontier
of France, 4 leagues from San Sebastian,
5 leagues from Bayonne.
16th July 1813.

DEAR BROTHER,

The day after we left our last encampment we moved into San
Estevan & stayed in quarters 3 fine days. The day before yesterday
at 10 in the morning we moved from our quarters & lay in a wood
just by till 3 o'clock and then marched by the river [Bidassoa]. The
road from thence to where we now are is on the side of the rocks
winding with the river & is exceedingly bad more than half the way.
In many places only one man could pass at once. Nearly the whole of
the way it rained as hard as ever I saw in England. I was completely
wet through. After marching $\frac{3}{4}$ of a league we halted on a hill. Got a
good fire & dried myself as well as I could. We marched at daylight
& it continued raining till 4 o'clock. We here came up with the
French and skirmished until dark when we got possession of half the
village of Vera & they had the other.[1] It contains two churches. Each
party had one. There was much brandy, indian corn &c. in the village.
We came upon them rather unexpectedly as in many of the houses
they had bread made which we took the liberty of putting in the oven
for them as they had not the time. During the skirmishing I was with

---

[1] Wellington's main effort at this time was devoted to the siege of San
Sebastian and 'it appeared to me to be desirable to obtain possession of the
débouchés of the mountains towards Vera . . . The enemy made but a trifling
resistance and withdrew their posts to the top of the Puerto [pass] de Vera.'

The bridge of Vera was the most practicable way by which the French
might turn the divisions which covered the approaches to San Sebastian on
the main road and the bridgehead across the Bidassoa which the Light
Division seized on 15 July made it very difficult for the French to advance
by this route. The casualties of the Forty Third on this day were twelve
wounded.

the colours (the place always of the 2nd senior ensign). One or more companies always remain with them in action. The river turns here & the heights at the turn are the French position & is very strong. We could see them very plain. The town is close to the river & steep hills near it. Behind these a range higher & beyond them others again more elevated, which divide France from Spain. The 95th, who are on a very high hill, can see a considerable distance into France.

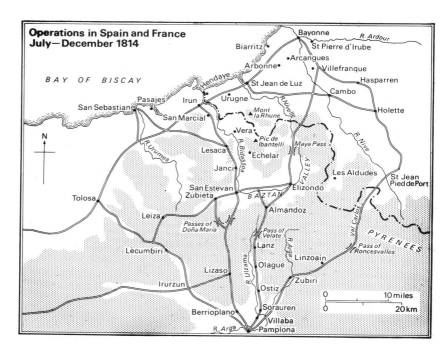

We lie by the river side. Longa (the guerrilla chief), with 5,000 men, is on the other side of the river. They commenced the skirmishing & were at it all day. I hope & think the Spaniards will fight well now. Longa's nephew told one of our officers that his men swore they would kill every Frenchman & destroy every town they came to in France but this will not be allowed as, two days ago, we had a General Order stating that, as we are going into an enemy's country, officers must be on the alert & that no one was to plunder, any more than in Spain, as it is not the people we make war upon, but the rulers of France. Commissaries to pay for provisions as in Spain.[1] So, in all probability, we go into France though we must wait the taking of San Sebastian. To go into France you have to go by a road 6 or 8 days' march in length, impassable for cannon & by throwing up redoubts on the heights one regiment may annoy a whole army.[2] The French took a vast quantity of corn from the village of Vera but it is the last they will have to sack. I hope they will not wait an attack but what can they do? If they retire, we follow them.

19th July. Nothing has transpired since the 16th. Just after writing our company was ordered for the outlying piquet when we marched to the top of one of the highest hills from whence I had a peep into France. The French were in possession of the valley below.

After marching along the top of the hill for a mile the main body of the picquet halted. The 7th Division [was] ½ a league beyond us. I was then ordered to take the advanced post with 24 men & moved on till we arrived at the last little hill from the valley, the French picquets [being] on the opposite one. We were near enough to call to each other. My Portuguese boy had a great deal of talk with one. After opening a communication with the 7th Division I lay down to rest and was awoke at day break by a cock crowing & fully intended to have him for dinner. However, Jack (the universal term for

---

[1] *General Order of 9 July 1813.* 'The officers and soldiers must recollect that their nations are at war with France solely because the Ruler of the French nation will not allow them to be at peace, and is desirous of forcing them to submit to his yoke: and they must not forget that the worst of the evils suffered by the enemy, in his profligate invasion of Spain and Portugal, have been occasioned by the irregularities of the soldiers and their cruelties, authorised and encouraged by their chiefs, towards the unfortunate and peaceful inhabitants of the country. To revenge this conduct on the peaceful inhabitants of France would be unmanly and unworthy of the nations to whom the Commander of the Forces now addresses himself and, at all events, would be the occasion of similar and worse evils to the army at large than those which the enemy's army have suffered in the Peninsula.'

[2] Hennell greatly exaggerates the difficulties of crossing the border into France. The main road into France by Irun is fairly level and, apart from the fact that the frontier bridge at Behobie had been destroyed, was perfectly practicable for all forms of transport. The subsidiary road over the Puerto de Vera is only seven or eight miles long before it rejoins the main road. It offered good defensive positions to the French but could not possibly take six or eight days' march.

Frenchmen) was there first for, on entering the house from which I heard him, I learned I was late by $\frac{1}{4}$ of an hour.

The French were driven out of the houses in the morning but not before they had completely stripped them. The country is very fine here & the houses large & good with gardens to all. Jack has not left us any ripe fruit or vegetables.

At 12 o'clock some of the inhabitants came in after 20 days' absence. They seemed fully prepared to see things as they were & were very little dejected. I got their good will completely by not allowing the foraging parties to cut the corn as there was plenty of grass. The valley below us runs into France though the main road is through the French position over the mountains. The French are continually blowing their trumpets & beating their drums. The French are very civil enemies for there is brandy selling at a house between the two sentinels & though they will not allow us to fetch it yet we may have it by means of the inhabitants. One of their men asked one of ours to buy some tobacco.

We can hear the cannonade going on at San Sebastian very plain. We are always most at ease when near the French. I was sorry to be relieved from my post. It is a beautiful sight to see the different fires on the hills at night. I hope we go into France for the sake of having to say so hereafter. It seems by the behaviour of the French that they do not expect to come back any more. Woe be to the inhabitants of the first French village the guerrillas get into, notwithstanding orders.

We are sick of the mountains. It rains every day almost & there is little forage. Our greatest comfort is plenty of wood & water. Most of the houses are 3 stories high. The upper one is open at the end in which they put the corn directly it is cut. The roof projects about a yard & there are balconies all along the fronts. If you sleep in a house you are sure to be covered with fleas, & if it is not of the better sort, lice also & it is two or three days after you get to camp before you get rid of them. The people here are more civil than any I have met with & all speak the Biscayan. It is only elderly people who talk Castilian as they call it, meaning Spanish.

Yours &c.
G.H.

LETTER XX

DEAR BROTHER,

The day after I last wrote our company was for outlying picquet at the village of Vera. The captain & one subaltern stayed at one end while I was detached to the other, $\frac{1}{2}$ a mile distant with half the company. The French had possession of the range of mountains formed by hills rising behind hills 4, 5 or 6 in number until covered by rocks with trees on them, so that a great force may be concealed. The lower hills about as steep & high as Greenwich Hill. I was in the street just under one [with] orchards adjoining, with walls ravines & trees, so that the French could come down unobserved within 3 or 4 yards of my sentinels and, if they chose, fire through their heads. They did fire at one of our officers the night before at dusk. I received instructions how to act from the preceding picquet. I placed my men on sentry all night & visited them 3 or 4 times. The French are by day about as far distant as from the top to the bottom of Greenwich Hill & at night sometimes run half way down. At ten o'clock in the morning a kine came running down the hill & two Frenchmen after it, endeavouring if possible to stop it but, after considerable difficulty, we made a prize of it. After having killed it, by shooting it, we divided the spoil very soon. I had half the fat, the kidney, tongue & hide for my share. I made a plumb pudding of the fat & covered my trunk with part of the hide.

The oldest inhabitant of these mountains says he never knew three days without rain in his life. It rained excessively on the 24th & 25th. Half the tents were in a swim. Three nights ago I rose with legs & arms wet through. There was an iron foundry just by me to which I went in the morning & dried myself in the blankets. The foundry is simple. It has two large rough bellows to smelt the ore in, a charcoal fire & has a large beam to beat it into bars, which is turned by water.

We heard the fire at San Sebastian very plain. On the 25th we heard an attempt had been made on San Sebastian & we lost 700 killed, wounded & prisoners. The whole grenadier company of the 1st Royals got into a house & fell through all the floors. Half the regiment are prisoners.[1]

Our sailors begged to be employed in one of the batteries. 10 or 12 came out to one[2] & soon after a shell alighted in the battery with the fuse still burning. One of them cried 'Heave it over, Jack!' & while in the act of doing so it burst & killed & wounded half of them.

After this a flag of truce was sent in to know how our prisoners were treated. They fared well & the wounded were well attended to. All hospitals in besieged towns are respected. A flag is placed on top. The French have put our wounded & prisoners in a house opposite the breach, so that if we fire at the breach the house will suffer.

On the 25th we moved one league backward. We heard that Genl. Hill had been attacked at Maya Pass with a superior force. We halted on top of one of the highest mountains. It rained all the way. It being in the midst of the clouds, we could not see three or four yards before us. At 5 o'clock it cleared up & we had a most beautiful view of the sea. Few forgot to say 'I wish I was upon you.'

The views here are beautiful, you see hills upon hills with villages & single houses scattered in the valleys (valleys themselves are hills), the gardens, orchards & corn around them (principally indian corn). The mountains are covered with brakes,[3] heath & grass. The next day, the 26th, we halted. No clouds over the sea tho' all the mountains

---

[1] An attempt to storm San Sebastian was made on 25 July and failed disastrously partly because the town, standing at the end of a narrow isthmus, was an extremely difficult place to attack and partly because the assault was ill-arranged and those taking part had little confidence in success. There were 563 casualties of whom six officers and 118 other ranks were taken prisoner. The bulk of the losses fell on the First Royal, who lost 331 officers and men. This regiment is better known as the Royal Scots but the designation Scots had only recently been reintroduced into their title and they were still predominantly made up of Irishmen and Englishmen.

[2] The Royal Navy had landed six short 24 pounders from HMS *Surveillante* together with two officers, five warrant officers and fifty seamen from HMS *Surveillante*, *Lyra* and *Sparrow* to assist in the siege.

[3] Brakes = bracken.

had them. The wind, as usual, N or N.W. It rained at dusk as I was preparing to go to bed, when orders came to march immediately & we set off through trees on a narrow winding road round the mountains. It continued raining all night. We crawled along not able to see the man next to us, till 2 o'clock, then began to descend, the men continually falling.

We had about 2 miles to descend & arrived in the valley 1½ miles from Sanesteban. We had not moved 2 leagues all night. We marched up the valley a league farther. I fell asleep several times on my horse. Our baggage did not march until daybreak & was 2 hours after us. Men & horses much fatigued. Next morning being a hot cloudy day, moved ½ a mile to a hill with trees, which movement took us two hours.

After getting my breakfast, I was for a court-martial which occupied me till 5 o'clock trying 16 prisoners for plundering &c. All except two were punished by flogging that night, each receiving 50 or 100 lashes. I do not now think it proper to give you my opinion upon flogging. Suffice it to say that I always bear in remembrance that I am accountable to a superior tribunal whose Judge has said 'Blessed are the merciful for they shall obtain mercy.' After this bloody parade, I had scarcely finished a bad meal &, with a heavy heart, when, ordering my servant to make my bed, 'March immediately' was the order. We moved immediately up the mountain, after being 1½ hours accoutred first, & then after crawling till one o'clock in the morning lay down to sleep 2 hours till daylight & then marched till 12 o'clock in the day with only a little bit of biscuit to eat & over tremendous mountains to this place.[1] We are under orders to march

---

[1] The heading of this letter is misleading. The Light Division was about 5 leagues from Pamplona but only in a roundabout way was it on the road from there to Bayonne. It was at Lecumberri on the road running north west from Pamplona to Tolosa. Quartermaster Surtees of the Ninety Fifth also describes the place as being 'on the great road from Bayonne to Pamplona'.

On the day that the assault on San Sebastian had failed the French had attacked in two large columns over the Maya and Roncesvalles passes aiming for Pamplona. As a precaution against their being successful Wellington had ordered the Light Division to march to the crest of the Sierra de Aralar to stop any possible French drive from Pamplona towards San Sebastian. It was a memorably difficult march and according to John Kincaid of the Rifles on one night they moved 'in utter darkness through a mountain path where, in many places, a false step might roll a fellow as far

at a moment's notice. There has been firing all day towards Pamplona. Soult took the command of the French 8 days since. He is an able & dashing general. I hear we have given them a good thrashing.[1]

> YOURS &c.
> G.H.

---

as the other world. The consequence was that, although we were kept on our legs during the whole of the night, we found when daylight broke that the tail of the column had not got a quarter of a mile from their starting-post.' (*Adventures in the Rifle Brigade*, p. 240 (1830).)

[1] Marshal Soult, who had gone to join the French army in Germany early in 1813, was despatched to command the Army of Spain (then back in France) as soon as Napoleon received the news of Vitoria. He took over the command on 12 July and, quickly reorganizing the Armies of Portugal, the South, the Centre and the North into a single body, launched an attack to try to relieve Pamplona. He got to within five miles of the place before he was repulsed at the first battle of Sorauren (28 July). Two days later, in the second battle, he was driven to a precipitate retreat.

LETTER XXI

Camp 1 mile E. of Vera, 4th August 1813.

DEAR BROTHER,

We have only received letters & papers up to the 1st July yet. Our army has seldom suffered such fatigues as it has done the last week or ten days. We have not had so much of it as the 7th & 4th Divisions. Soult as Regent of Spain[1] attacked us with 50,000 men, determined to relieve Pamplona. With a very superior force he attacked the Pass of Maya &, after a severe repulse, took it & pushed on with provisions towards Pamplona & got within 3 leagues of it when our army attacked.[2]

We (the Light Division) were, as you will see by my last, making forced marches to get on & secure the main road. My baggage did not come up to us on the 30th & I sent back my other horse for it. It arrived next day with the poor animals quite knocked up, so I had to walk. At 3 o'clock we marched back 2 leagues.

[On] 1st August I was for the baggage [guard]. It was said we were going to the place we came from 3 nights before, near San Esteban which was 4½ leagues over the Pyrenees, a very severe march. It was dreadfully hot. A mile forward I found the baggage animals. I halted and refreshed for I was left behind, my horse having knocked up. I sent forward all that could go & remained all night with the rest, had plenty to eat & a good night's sleep. I needed it for I was nearly knocked up. How the poor fellows with knapsacks,

---

[1] Soult's instructions entitled him as the emperor's 'Lieutenant General in Spain'.

[2] The column with which Soult set out to relieve Pamplona through the Pass of Roncesvalles was 34,000 strong. His second column, which attacked through the Maya, was almost 21,000 strong. It is not surprising that Hennell should not have realized that the column which went over the Maya was not the same one which got close to Pamplona.

canteens,[1] havresacks, accoutrements, 60 rounds of ball cartridge & a firelock marched 3 leagues further I cannot conceive. Many were obliged to fall out & several died by the road.[2]

Next morning I got my horse on to the bottom of this mountain & halted the baggage for orders & walked up the mountain as fast as I could as I heard our regiment were going to attack a mountain while the 4th Division attacked another. The firing had commenced & just as I arrived they were rattling away. I found it was the mountain the 7th Division occupied previous to retiring. It is on the right of the valley leading from Vera into France & divided France from Spain. I arrived at one wing of our regiment which was a support half way up the mountain, at the time they were pushing up. It is the highest of the mountains near here. The clouds hung about it so that they could not see 20 yards.

The French had not many troops on it, nor did they need them. Half a regiment ought to defend it against 5 or 6 for it rises very steep to a point. The French made one or two charges. The 95th behaved most gallantly. Many of them crawled up the rocks amongst numbers of the enemy & were pushed over them & rolled down the mountain. They took hold of the belts of some & dashed them down the rocks.

---

[1] Canteen was the term used for the troops' wooden waterbottle.

[2] On 1 August the Light Division was ordered to make a forced march from Leyza to Sumbilla in order to cut off the retreat of Soult's army. The order should have reached them earlier and by the time they approached their destination it could be seen that they were too late so General Alten decided to push on to the bridge at Yanci where the first brigade (including the Forty Third) succeeded in inflicting heavy losses on the French rearguard by firing at them across the narrow gorge of the Bidassoa where 'we overlooked the enemy within a stone's throw, and from the summit of a precipice : the river separated us : but the French were wedged in a narrow road, with rocks enclosing them on one side and the river on the other.' (Cooke.) This was a remarkable march. Although its length was only about twenty five miles on the map it was over 'the rugged asperities of a prodigious mountain, the by-path of which was composed of overlapping slabs or rock, or stepping stones'. It was accomplished in nineteen hours, much of it under a blazing sun. Several accounts mention that some men actually died during this march : there is no record that any actually did. Two writers who were present state that 200 men fell out in some unspecified regiment (not their own). The only firm figure is that in 3rd battalion Ninety Fifth Rifles only nine men (out of five companies) fell out.

Notwithstanding all these tremendous disadvantages they [the French] were driven from the pinnacle & down into France.[1]

During this the 4th Division were attacking a mountain to our right that formed a chain of 3 hills. We had 2 & they were defending the last & highest. We were about a mile off with two ravines between us so that we could not see them from behind the mountain. They [the French] had 2 square bodies behind it & kept up a fire till dark when the 17th Portuguese relieved us & we came back to camp.

We turned out next morning an hour before day break & at day light marched round the mountain till our first company was in France. It being then light & a fine day we saw they had all left so we turned back to our camp. Lord March came up & ordered us to turn out at a moment's warning. We turned out this morning before day break (the custom when near the enemy) but we had no orders yet. The enemy expected all day yesterday; they were under arms waiting for us. Our troops are all moving up so it is probable we shall attack them soon. Lord Wellington is in high spirits & particularly pleased with his troops.

So we are now on the borders of France, with a force not able to stand before us. It is a most beautiful situation. We can see the enemy fall in & hear their drums & trumpets distinctly. It is an old soldier's remark & very true that we are never so much at ease as when near the enemy.

In going down towards Pamplona the inhabitants were leaving their houses with all they could carry on their heads, going into the mountains to hide themselves. It is very distressing & one wd. think be sufficient to raise any nation except Spaniards. They returned in 3 days as we did and then we saw a number of stout well-made fellows with their arms folded lounging about the place or gaping out of windows, as unconcerned as possible. One of them came to me with the baggage & desired me to see how they [the French] had ransacked his house. I asked him why he had not a firelock and did not join some Spanish regiment & assist in driving the French out. The

---

[1] This was the attack on the Pic d'Ibantelli (638 metres), which is just within the French frontier, north of Echalar. It should have been impregnable but the French were demoralized after their repulse and retreat. One of the Rifle officers who took part described it as 'the most gentleman-like day's fighting that I ever experienced'. The British suffered only 27 casualties of which one man wounded was in the Forty Third.

fellow pursed up his lip, shrugged his shoulders & sneaked off like a Spaniard (a proud Castillian). Just after the other brigade took some prisoners & baggage near the Ebro, as we were passing a village, the inhabitants were calling out *'Viva Ingleses'*. A young lad, a French prisoner, said they said just so when they came through. At one place in the country they mistook us for French troops and were loudly calling out *'Viva Franceses'*.

Tho' the troops have been much fatigued lately, to Lord Wellington's credit they have been well supplied with rations. We get excellent biscuit.[1]

Yours &c.
G.H.

---

[1] A somewhat surprising comment since the division received no rations between dawn on 31 July and midday on 2 August. According to John Cooke the troops were so weak before the attack on the Ibantelli 'that they could hardly stand; however an excellent commissary had managed to overtake us and hastily served out half a pound of biscuit to each individual, which the soldiers devoured while in the act of priming and loading as they moved on to the attack'.

7 On the Frontier

Between the end of the battle of the Pyrenees in early August and the beginning of October Wellington made no attempt to invade France. Not only were San Sebastian and Pamplona still in French hands but he was still waiting for the Royal Navy to bring reinforcements and supplies from Lisbon to his new base at Pasajes. Equally enjoining delay was the need for news from eastern Europe. If peace was made at the Prague conference (see note 1 on p. 121), Napoleon would be able to bring overwhelming forces to the Pyrenees and the allied army would have to retrace its march to Portugal.

After a bloody storming San Sebastian fell on 31 August, the day on which Soult made a last attempt to relieve it. On 11 September news came from the French lines that the war in the east had been renewed with Austria now among France's enemies. Only Pamplona now remained of the obstacles to a further advance and Wellington was prepared to make a limited advance even before it fell. His aim was to capture 'the heights on the right of the Bidassoa [which] command such a view of us that we must have them, and the sooner the better'. He hoped to attack on 23 September but the Chief Engineer 'is not certain that the orders he sent have reached the officers in charge [of the pontoon train at Vitoria] and he has taken no measures to repeat them. He put his letter into the Spanish post office, I conclude directed in English, and without knowing whether the officer in charge of the pontoons is in communication with that post office.' The delay in bringing up the bridging equipment meant that the advance had to be postponed until 7 October.

When it came the attack was completely successful. The Fifth Division splashed across the estuary of the Bidassoa on fords the French believed not to exist and captured Hendaye with hardly a shot fired. The First Division crossed with little more opposition on their right and further to the east the Light Division and some Spaniards captured the southern part of the dominating massif of La Grande Rhune. The French were taken by surprise and, as one of their generals remarked that evening, 'Our troops fight badly and are worthless. Only disgrace can be expected with such men.' At a cost of less than 1,600 casualties Wellington had opened the door into France.

LETTER XXII

Heights near Vera, 10th August 1813.

DEAR BROTHERS,

Nothing has occurred since we drove the French from the hill on our right. The French occupy the same position in front of us. The weather has been fine since we came here this time. As we are within sight of France it is most likely we shall go there or into quarters near here. Either will suit me, but the former much the best. I am anxious for more news from the north. If the armistice is broken I hope we shall soon compel the French Emperor to make an honourable peace.[1] In that case I suppose that those subalterns who have been 3, 4 or 5 years in this country, enduring great hardships & injuring their healths, will be allowed, I might say compelled, to retire upon the grand allowance of half pay, an ensign 1/10d & a lieutenant 2/4d per day.[2]

Our company is on one of the highest hills to observe the movements of the enemy, so I have amused myself thus. [A blank space in the surviving copy of this letter indicates where Hennell drew a sketch map which is now missing.—Ed.]

There are 2 roads over the pass, Nos. 1 & 2. The enemy's principal

---

[1] After some inconclusive fighting in eastern Germany Napoleon had agreed to the Armistice of Pleischwitz on 4 June. A peace conference met at Prague but, since France was not prepared to make any meaningful concessions, the war on that front (known both in England and in the Peninsula as 'the north') was resumed on 17 August but with Austria joined to Russia and Prussia as Napoleon's enemies. News of the end of the armistice did not reach Wellington until 11 September when he read it in a captured French newspaper. It had reached London on 27 August but adverse winds prevented it being forwarded to Spain.

[2] The concept of an emergency commission was unknown at this time and the extra officers taken on during the war (when the establishment of British officers rose from 3,107 to 10,590) were entitled to the meagre allowance of half (actually third) pay for the rest of their lives.

force 3 & 4. No. 5 the sea. The village is Vera 6. French pickets, 7 is a battery. To the right there is a mountain that declines into a valley from whence we see 2 or 3 leagues into France. 10 a battery, 11 a house fortified, 12 the river. We have the valley & village.

I hear a fleet is just arrived so I hope to have things reasonable. I was at Lesaca (head quarters) yesterday & paid 4lb Irish butter 4/6d, sugar, bread 1/-d per lb. I bought some mackerel, very small, & had them pickled. These things may appear trifling to you but had your jaws been as often sprung open again in endeavouring to chew tough beef as mine, you would think it a real treat to have some fish slip easily down your throat that had been used to bolting for months. It is a delightful day & we seem as much at our ease as possible though perhaps in 5 minutes we may be put in motion & commence fighting. In these mountains a soldier's life is varied indeed.

13th August. I am the officer on the look out station & as I have just sent off the morning report here is a copy of it. 'The enemy has made no movement.' 7 o'clock. There has been a heavy fog in the valley these two hours. Above a certain height it is perfectly clear. It is a beautiful sight & appears as though the valley were only just under the clouds.

20th August. We have no movement or alteration since. We are still on the hill this side Vera. The French on the one on the opposite side.

Allow me to request that none of my letters may appear in newspapers. What nonsense & lies do foolish officers write to their friends who put them into the newspapers. One blockhead said that in the battle of Vitoria the 3rd, Light, 4th & 7th divisions fought hand to hand. Another that it was the most obstinately contested battle ever fought. Another that on the evening, when they were plundering, it rained excessively hard. It did rain a drop. One letter said we were besieging, & he believed we had taken, Bayonne. Pray, has no fool told you that Paris is in danger & that from good authority he believes it will be taken ?[1]

---

[1] Wellington frequently issued orders requesting officers to be careful in what they wrote in letters home. 'He has frequently lamented the ignorance which has appeared in the opinions communicated in letters written from the army, and the indiscretion with which those letters are published.' (GO of 10 August 1810.) However, he believed censorship to be unthinkable. As he wrote to the Prime Minister, 'I am sure that your lordship does not

BATTLE OF THE PYRENEES. July 28th 1813

Between the combined Armies, under the command of the Duke of Wellington, and the French under Marshall Soult.

The battle of the Pyrenees; action at Sorauren, 28 July 1813
(*National Army Museum*)

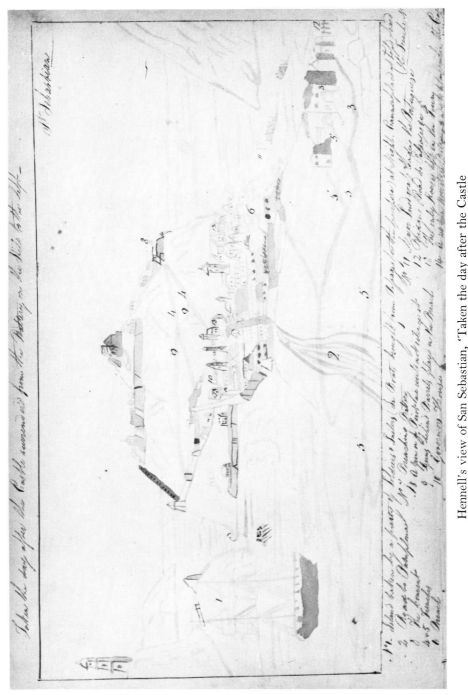

Hennell's view of San Sebastian, 'Taken the day after the Castle surrendered from the Battery on the Hills to the left'

I hope we shall not be upon these hills in the wet season. Should we winter here we shall be able to get good accommodation & eatables as we are so near the coast.

27th August. The reports here vary every day. One day 'War! War!' another 'Peace' is the cry. If peace takes place, we shall hear of it from the French first. The flags of truce they send in all say they expect an early peace. In the wet season, which the inhabitants say will set in in about three weeks, the roads are impassable. Forage is getting very scarce. Our bâtman went up to the French position yesterday. Their picket made a great noise about it. They, our men, did not, however, desist, till they got a load.

28th August. An order has just arrived for 100 men, 2 captains, 4 subalterns for the storming party at San Sebastian. This is one of the highest honours the division could have received. Of course, the same division will be employed as before – viz : the 5th. The senior officer of each rank always has the choice. Our officers were called together & the colonel told us the business. The senior captain was not present but came up during the time of the conference. The Col. said, 'Captain Brock, we are to give the storming party at San Sebastian tonight. Several captains wish to go. Will you allow it, being senior?' He said, 'No, sir, I will go myself.' Lieuts. John O'Connell & [John] Cooke are gone with him. The regiment had 30 men & 2 sergeants to give. Although Capt. Brock did not know one minute before, he determined on going without hesitation. Two subalterns present declined. This is not esteemed a shadow of a disgrace. This is John O'Connell's third time, 1st at Ciudad Rodrigo, 2nd Badajoz. When an officer offers on a service of this kind it is done without any bombast; they look serious and pale. The act tells this is not from fear. I have just wished them good bye as they passed and did so exactly as you would have taken leave of a person going to the play. The sergeants have been nearly quarrelling, saying, 'I have been on 1 & 2 (some of them 3), why may I not go on this?'

---

expect that I, or any other officer in command of a British army, can pretend to prevent the correspondence of the officers with their friends', and had to resign himself to the fact that 'we are the most indefatigable writers of letters that exist in the world . . . As soon as an accident happens, every man who can write, and has a friend who can read, sits down to write an account of what he does not know, and his comments on what he does not understand.'

You may suppose this is for appearance before their comrades, I sincerely believe it is *not*. The men are equally so. There was so many chosen from the company I pay and the quarrel lasted ten minutes. Who should be rejected?

29th August. Tomorrow San Sebastian is to be stormed. Only Lieut. O'Connell is allowed to go from our regiment as there were seniors in others. Major Napier,[1] Capt. Brock & Lieut. Cooke [were not chosen]. Lord Wellington's letter to General Alten was highly complimentary. He stated he wanted 1 field officer, 2 captains, 4 subalterns & 100 men of the Light Division to show the 5th Division the way into the breach.[2] I have no doubt they will do it. The officers gone are:—Lieut. Col. Hunt, 52nd, Capt. Anderson, 52nd, Capt. ...... [sic], Lieut. Perceval, 95th, O'Connell, 43rd, Lieut. ...... [sic], 3rd Batt. 95th, Lieut. ...... [sic], 52nd.[3]

6th Sept. 1813. It is surprising we have had so little fighting while all around us have had so much. We have had as much marching & it is mere chance we have not had as much fighting & by what follows you will see that we have been nearer to it in this last attack of Soult's than any yet.

I wrote you we gave 1 lieut., 2 sergeants & 30 men to the storming

---

[1] William Napier, then a brevet major, had been promised the command of the stormers but Brevet Lieutenant Colonel Hunt of the Fifty Second asserted his right as senior to the command. Napier appealed to Wellington, who refused to interfere. Being determined to go at all costs he took a musket and paraded in the ranks. He was spotted by General Alten and ordered back to his regiment.

[2] Wellington wrote to the First, Fourth and Light Divisions for parties of volunteers 'to show the Fifth Division how to mount a breach'. Not unnaturally this was bitterly resented by the Fifth, already smarting from their repulse in July and the volunteers were not allowed to form the Storming Party. Nevertheless it was they who eventually broke into the town.

[3] Hennell's list of the Light Division's officer volunteers is incomplete and, in one case, inaccurate. The list should read:

B/Lt. Col. John Hunt, 52nd. (wounded)
Capt. Robert Campbell, 52nd. (wounded)
Lieut. John O'Connell, 43rd. (killed)
Lieut. Augustus Harvest, 52nd. (killed)
Lieut. James Perceval, 95th. (wounded)
Lieut. Charles Eaton, 95th.
2/Lieut. William Hamilton, 95th. (wounded)

party of San Sebastian. Poor O'Connell was wounded by a grape shot in the thigh and a sergeant wished to carry him off but he would not allow it for, he said, as both the sergeants were wounded the men would have no one to lead them on. Very soon he received a musket ball in the belly. One of the sergeants was shot in the nose, the other (it seems Kilpatrick received a ball in his hand close by me at the battle of Salamanca) has now lost his hand.[1] 5 privates were killed, 14 wounded, so that of 33 only 10 escaped. Lieut. [Augustus] Harvest of the 52nd was killed at San Sebastian. They were fine young men.

We had a detachment coming to join & 2 officers with it, Jones & Folliet. They met the French & gained the 7th Division. One of our sergeants saw a Frenchman firing from a tree. He fired & brought him down. The party were behind a wall. Folliet said he would see if there were any more & very imprudently exposed himself at a gap in the wall. He immediately received a shot in the belly. The detachment had no other wounded or killed.[2]

I must now give you some hearsay particulars of San Sebastian. It was so strong a place, so admirably defended & so boldly taken. Major Snodgrass of the Portuguese service led the men through water breast high under a tremendous fire of grape & cannister. Our fellows did not go first but pushed forward &, I believe, were first in the town. The troops were 2 hours in the breach. There are various opinions on the propriety of remaining so long in the breach. I am not competent to give one. A mine blew up too soon & killed many of the enemy, upon which our men dashed into the town & fought

---

[1] Five sergeants of the Forty Third took part in the storming, three of them presumably serving as temporary privates. All five were subsequently promoted to the newly created rank of colour sergeant. The two 'official' sergeants were William Kilpatrick, who lost an arm, and Thomas Blood, severely wounded. Blood was given an ensign's commission in Sixth Foot on 10 November and became a lieutenant on 8 September 1814.

[2] Soult launched an attempt to relieve San Sebastian on the day on which it was stormed. His main attack fell on the Spaniards (see note 1 on p. 127) but one brigade of Seventh Division was passed behind the Light Division and had a sharp engagement at Zalain de Lesaca where they suffered nearly 300 casualties. Folliet and his detachment would have passed close to this fighting on their way to the regiment from the port of Pasajes where they landed. According to the regimental history four men of the regiment were also killed in this action.

until the French retired into the castle, which still holds out tho' it most likely will fall in a day or two.[1]

I will now give you some account of what I saw of Soult's bold attack to relieve it. In this, the sketch I sent you will be of service. The night before everything was as usual. Just before turning in at daylight the assembly sounded & we found the hill just over Vera covered with troops defiling down to the river, leaving the village on their left. There were various opinions as to their numbers. I think from 30 to 40,000 men.

10th Sept. You will see in the sketch I sent you that the river makes a turn just where it leaves the paper. It was [there] they forded it, drove the Spaniards away & took possession of the bridge. The Spaniards had thrown up works on the other, which of course they took possession of. During the night they brought cannon on the hill & they now opened on our left brigade (the 43rd are on the right, commanded by General [James] Kempt), about 12 or 14 pieces of cannon, these covered their fording. [They] then filed down the hill, crossed the river, formed into brigades & divisions & then moved up the mountains towards San Sebastian. They were, from 8 o'clock in the morning till 2, crossing, during this we heard a heavy fire towards St [Jean de] Luz. They left a division to guard the bridge. The 4th Division moved the night before from Lesaca to the heights they wished to pass. So you see it was a bold manoeuvre. He concentrated near 50,000 men & while part were attempting to force the Bidassoa near the sea, the others pushed between the Light and 4th Divisions.

---

[1] The second storm of San Sebastian on 31 August was almost as unsuccessful as the first had been. It cost the allied army 2,000 casualties of whom 500 died. When it seemed that the main assault was halted Kenneth Snodgrass, a captain in the Fifty Second serving as a major in the Portuguese army, led one and a half Portuguese battalions across the Urumea estuary, which was waist deep at low tide, in an attempt to reach a smaller breach. Eventually the siege guns reopened close over the heads of the stormers and set fire to a collection of explosive and combustible materials stored on the wall for use against the attack and under cover of the confusion caused the British were able to break into the town. They were fortunate that a mine containing 12 cwt of gunpowder which had been dug under the breach failed to explode.

The castle of San Sebastian, on a rock at the seaward tip of the town, was bombarded and surrendered on 9 September.

The Bidassoa was defended by Spanish troops alone & it is with great pleasure I have to say that they behaved most gallantly. They retired from a hill for the sole purpose of enticing the French on, which answered as they came in front of the hill, within pistol shot distance, gave them a steady volley, came to the port, regularly advanced. When they came within 4 or 5 paces, came down to the charge &, with great loss, bayonetted the French down the hill. I look upon this as a matter of great importance & think it adds considerably to the probability of the peace of Spain.[1]

It is impossible for troops to have behaved better than the Portuguese did in advancing to the breach of San Sebastian. They were up to the middle in water, grape, cannon & musquetry mowing down full $\frac{1}{2}$ of the first regiment that advanced and yet they did not hurry or spread, but marched regularly to the breach with Major Snodgrass at their head to the admiration of all the spectators. See what our example & instruction have done. 5 years ago 100 French would have driven 1,000 of these troops before them like sheep.[2] The Spanish troops are increasing daily.

But to proceed with my narrative. The brigade of the 7th Division opposed the French at the top of the hill & kept the pass [of Vera]. Ours remained quiet spectators of it the whole day. At dusk we moved nearer Lesaca, one wing[3] taking possession of a height beyond them.

---

[1] Soult's attack was made with 50,000 men across a number of fords in the Bidassoa between Hendaye and Endalazza. The main weight of the attack fell on 6,000 Spaniards drawn up on the crest of the hill of San Marcial who repulsed two powerful French assaults, the first substantial Spanish victory since Bailen in 1808. At one stage their commander, General Giron, sent to Wellington for British help but he refused saying that 'if I send you English troops, they will win the battle; but as the French are already in retreat you may as well win it for yourselves'. He later reported that the conduct of the Spaniards 'was equal to that of any troops I have ever seen engaged'.

[2] See also note 1 on p. 126. In 1809 Major General William Carr Beresford had been appointed commander in chief of the Portuguese army with the rank of marshal, Wellington being marshal general. With the assistance of a liberal supply of seconded British officers Beresford had trained them up until they were fit to take their place in the line with the British. By 1813 Wellington could say that, 'no troops could behave better; that they never had a notion of turning; and that nothing could equal their forwardness and ready willing tempers'.

[3] A wing was half a battalion, five companies.

It began to rain as we moved & continued raining all night. It is very strange that for 2 or 3 years we have never engaged but it has thundered, lightened & rained the night before. The men are getting quite superstitious. One of the officers asked the sentry if anything had occurred. He said 'No' but he was sure there would be tomorrow. He was right.

There was one house where we bivouacked & the colonel politely asked all the officers in, & let the men get into a large stable. The colonel allowed half our officers to go & see San Sebastian stormed (for which he was heartily sorry) so that I had to leave the house & take charge of the outlying picket. I had my boat cloak on & was as hot & wet with perspiration as possible. We procured some wine & I deliberately got so tipsy that I did not know when I lay down to sleep. I had a violent headache.

In the morning it was fine. We were to have marched & to have attacked the French but they, being repulsed at the river, retired by the same road. The river was very much swollen & the 95th gave them a very warm reception at the bridge & killed one, if not two or three generals there. Could we have destroyed that bridge, Lord Wellington says we should have had every man of them. So that at daylight they were going up the hill again & we had just got back to see them.[1]

I not only give the following remark as my own but many wiser have made it : 'We are much too careful of our guns.' We had none

---

[1] There was heavy rain on the afternoon of the day of the battle of San Marcial and the Bidassoa rose so that much of the French army was trapped on the south bank of the river. Ten thousand men under General Vandermaesen had no way of escape except by the bridge at Vera, fifty yards long and 'not wide enough for more than three or four to pass abreast'. At the far end in some loop-holed houses were 70 men of the Rifles under Captain Daniel Cadoux. The French managed to kill the two sentries but could make no progress across the bridge under rifle fire at close range. If Cadoux had been reinforced he could have held his position all night but his brigadier, Skerrett, ordered him to retire. Cadoux queried the order, saying that his men were in no danger. Skerrett, however, repeated the order and Cadoux complied, remarking that 'but few of the party would reach camp'. In the withdrawal he and 16 men were killed, the other officers and 43 men were wounded. General Vandermaesen was among the large number of French killed in the action.

here. Could we have had Ross's brigade of light pieces,[1] we might have annoyed them in passing the river. There is certainly hazard in having them [guns] in such a country as this but what would it have signified if we had lost one or two.

The castle of San Sebastian, after having more shells burst over it than any other place in the world it is supposed, surrendered yesterday morning, 2 o'clock so that we have now only Pamplona on this side of the kingdom.[2]

The great question is 'Will Soult again make an effort to relieve it?' Many say he will by passing near Jaca.[3] We have now 2 more divisions at liberty, the 1st & the 5th.[4] It has been very wet & the roads are getting bad & we are throwing up works in most of them so I, for one, think he will not. A spy was taken up yesterday with a letter [rolled] in a quill to the Governor of Pamplona from Soult saying he was sorry he could not see him on the 18th but he hoped he should soon. I see the 4th Division, which was covering headquarters yesterday, is moved. So is the 7th & I sincerely hope we shall move directly from these hills. We lie just on the summit & last night it rained in torrents & the wind blew tremendously. By placing a blanket on the westward side of my tent it did not blow down & I was dry.

YOURS &C.
G.H.

---

[1] B/Lt. Col. Hew Dalrymple Ross commanded A (the Chestnut) Troop, Royal Horse Artillery which usually supported the Light Division. On the day of the battle his troop had been ordered from their station at Andoain to Irun to oppose the right of the French attack.

[2] Pamplona was not starved into surrender until 30 October. The French also held the coastal fortress of Santoña until the end of the war. On the east coast Marshal Suchet still held much of Catalonia but this had been annexed to France.

[3] The pass of Jaca (Puerto de Somport) is more than 60 miles inland and the main road from it led to Saragossa. There was a very minor road by which Pamplona could have been reached with immense trouble.

[4] The Fifth Division had been engaged in the siege of San Sebastian. The First had been covering the siege and faced the estuary of the Bidassoa.

LETTER XXIII

DEAR BROTHERS,

Annexed is a sketch of San Sebastian, or more properly the ruins of it for it is all destroyed except 4 or 5 houses. After it was taken it was suffered to burn for none of our soldiers showed the least inclination to put out the fire but suffered it to burn, keeping steady to their only object, plunder. Our surgeon says the scene was shocking – many females wounded, some leaping from the top of houses on fire, &c. It *was* a beautiful town.[1] It is a very strong place &, its having the sea, an important one. It is repairing fast. As to Pamplona, reports vary so much as to prove you know as much about it as I do. You must not pay any attention to letters in the papers from officers here. All officers here laugh at them exceedingly.

I have been twice up the hill we took [Ibantelli] 'proudly to overlook their fertile valleys'. I saw the cathedral in Bayonne very plain & most of the town. The Pyrenees form a hilly half circle; the Maya pass in the centre. Every hill has troops on it in huts. We see them exercising (with glasses) as plain as if we commanded. Some seem as if we could throw stones upon them. Both of us are throwing up works.

No movement has taken place since my last. Since the stormy night when my horse died we have had fine weather. Report now says October is the finest month in the year. We have a report that a battle has been fought between the French & Austrians. The

---

[1] Lt. Col. William Gomm, A.Q.M.G., 5th Division, wrote, 'San Sebastian's is a more melancholy story than either that of Badajoz or Rodrigo . . . With the exception of ten or twelve fortunate buildings there is nothing left but the walls of its houses, and these are falling every instant with a tremendous crash.' (Gomm *op. cit.*, 319.) Gomm believed that the French had fired the town. Many Spaniards believed that San Sebastian was deliberately destroyed by the British because of its importance as a trading port.

French picquet sent over a day or two since extracts from their *Bulletins*, printed one side in French, the other English, others one Spanish, one Portuguese, which state vaguely that the French have killed & taken 80,000.[1]

I very much want a work on martial law. All officers are much too ignorant of it.

The Spanish troops are improving every day. For my part I have no fear of the French relieving Pamplona. The passes are ready to receive Soult whenever he thinks proper to approach them. He is universally allowed to be the first general Buonaparte has.

The forage for our horses is getting very short. It is rather strange I think that no English sutlers have come here yet. They would be well paid for we give 6d an onion, 2/-d a lb sugar, 4/-d lb butter, 3½ dollars per lb. tea, 3/-d coffee &c.

Soult says the French have made us good soldiers by example. So they have but unfortunately for them (like Mr Hennell teaching me chess) they have taught us rather too long & we beat them in every game. I heard an officer remark the other day that Old Douro (Lord W)[2] is a much better genl. now than he was at Salamanca. He learned much at Vitoria. A painter is at headquarters sketching a group for publication in which is a most excellent likeness of Lord Wellington.[3] You wd. be pleased to see how affable & polite

---

[1] This refers to the battle of Dresden (26–7 August) where the Austrians and Prussians were repulsed by Napoleon with the loss of 38,000 men. Two days after Hennell's letter Wellington was writing of another French report, 'It must be observed of these bulletins that they are printed at Bayonne, and are improvements on the lies even of the *Moniteur* [the French official newspaper].'

[2] Wellington was known to all ranks as Douro or Beau Douro from his second title, Baron Douro of Wellesley. Gleig recalled how, when his battalion arrived in Spain 'there were some in the ranks who had served during some of the earlier campaigns; these instantly recognized their old leader and the cry of *Douro! Douro!*, the familiar title given him by the soldiers was raised. This was followed by reiterated shouts to which he replied by taking off his hat and bowing.' (*The Subaltern*, p. 69 (1825).)

[3] The artist Thomas Heaphy was with headquarters to work on a group picture of Wellington and his staff which is now in the Mauritshuis and the watercolour sketches are in the National Portrait Gallery. He also did commissioned portraits at forty, later fifty guineas. This, said Larpent 'for a little water colour whole length; but he has taken twenty six and some excessively like.' (Larpent *op. cit.*, 278.)

he is on passing a group of officers. He is almost always dressed in his grey great coat. His lordship has ordered John O'Connell's ensigncy to be sold for the benefit of his mother, who is a widow.[1]

I pay a company, the emolument is from £40 to £50 per annum after paying the sergeant. It is paid half yearly & it is ½ year in arrears.[2] I mean to let mine remain to furnish my barrack room in England when I return. I shall be a lieutenant soon & then, instead of 30, shall have 40 dollars per month.[3] In reply to Magrath's question, when I am a lieut. I shall belong to the 2nd Batt.,[4] but no officer is allowed to go home, except thro' ill-health & being in the 2nd batt. & being 4 or 5 years here & then only when we have a great number of the same rank here & in winter quarters to return in 2 or 3 months. Besides I have no idea of returning till the regiment does. Tho' we have had a severe campaign, we hope to have a

---

[1] It was very unusual for a commission to be offered for sale other than by the holder. Not being heritable property, commissions lapsed on the death of the purchaser but the Duke of York, as Commander in Chief, was occasionally prepared to allow one to be sold for the dependants of an outstanding officer. This was done in the case of Major General Le Marchant when he was killed at Salamanca leaving a large and penurious young family. The regulation price of an ensign's commission in the infantry of the line was £400.

[2] This was the contingent allowance payable to captains of companies for acting as paymasters to their companies. 'In the absence of the captains, the subaltern officer appointed to the command of the troop or company is entitled to the contingent allowance for the time being.' (General Regulations & Orders for the Army, 12 August 1811, p. 95.)

[3] Hennell was now second ensign by seniority (see Appendix 2) and there were two vacant lieutenancies due to the deaths of Folliet and O'Connell. Promotion to lieutenant would increase his pay from 5/3d to 7/6d a day.

[4] According to the regulations all the senior officers of each rank served in the first battalion and their juniors in the second (or subsequent) battalions. Thus on promotion Hennell should have returned to England to join the 2nd battalion Forty Third which was stationed at Hythe, Kent. It was a system which caused great inconvenience more particularly when battalions were stationed in India and newly promoted officers had to spend six months on the voyage from one battalion to the other. Wellington was constantly pressed from the Horse Guards to release newly promoted officers to their proper battalions but usually managed to evade doing so until they were replaced from England.

comfortable winter here & the houses are superior to those at Gallegos.[1]

The Times is a high treat indeed. Major Napier says Vetus is a fool & that he is an officer on half-pay in Wales. He is a violent anti-ministerialist & detests *The Times*.[2] We have a fine opportunity to improve in politics as we generally read the prophecies after we know the event. Our officers have changed *The Statesman* for *The Courier*; it is to me jalap for salts.[3]

Our life here is a very idle one. Parade in the evening – so do the French. We see each other & hear their band playing. The beautiful valleys begin to look dull. All the corn is gone, the apple trees stripped long ago. The walnuts were scarce ripe before all were gone & the chestnuts are going fast. You can have no idea what destruction & waste an army carries with it. We are like locusts, every place we halt at, much more where we stay, bears marks of it &, altho' orders & punishments abound, it is impossible to prevent pillage. If a soldier wants a piece of wood to boil his kettle & there is a beautiful peach or apple by the side of a chestnut or oak, I do not believe he would go a yard to choose. I have seen fellows knock down a peck of unripe plums for the sake of eating 5 or 6. Houses fare no better than orchards. Bedsteads, chairs tables [all are taken for firewood] & in short it is what comes first, or if a man wants a bit of iron to screw his musket [he will use] a lock that has cost the owner several days' labour if at hand.

---

[1] Gallegos, north east of Fuentes de Oñoro and on the road from Ciudad Rodrigo to Portugal, had been the Forty Third's winter quarters in 1812–13.

[2] William Napier, as befitted a grandson of that extreme Whig the 3rd Duke of Richmond, was a lifelong radical and very scornful of the government, 'Oh! the wonderful works of Lords Bathurst [Secretary for War] and Liverpool [Prime Minister]' he wrote to his wife on the day after this letter was written.

Vetus was a pale imitation of Junius forty years earlier. According to Larpent, Wellington 'thought he knew the author, and that he had been in India. He went on to say that he did not think much of Vetus's letters: that many of his facts as to this country [Spain] were quite without foundation; that Vetus [did not know] anything about the war here, and what could or could not be done.' (*op. cit.*, 100.) It was generally believed that Vetus was James Macintosh, MP for Nairn, and recently returned from an Indian judgeship (though Wellington denied it was him). Another theory was that the writer was the Marquess of Wellesley, Wellington's elder brother.

[3] Jalap=a purgative.

I would not have my head in his place for all Lord Wellington's honours. The inhabitants being so rapacious does not lessen the inclination the men have to destroy. If you attempt to reason with them, their answer is 'It is the fortunes of war. Besides, who are for the damned Spaniards? They rob you when they can.' I hope Englishmen will never know by experience what it is to see their houses & property so treated. Spaniards in a measure deserve it. At the same time I am endeavouring to raise a mound of interest & curiosity [among my correspondents]. I am trying to find some solid stones towards a building of respect in which, if I live to return, I may walk & find a cordial reception & some of the most solid enjoyments we have in this world. The only means I have of giving you pleasure is the simple one of giving you information. I am quite well. The cold & slight rheumatism I had has left me.

YOURS &c.
G.H.

LETTER XXIV

Heights midway between Vera & St. Jean de Luz
13th Oct. 1813.

DEAR BROTHERS,

I received yesterday *The Times* to the 27th September. Except you were here, gaping for news like trout on a summer evening as we are, you cannot well conceive the pleasure it gives me.

I shall now give you a few particulars of the taking of the position I am now writing from. On the 6th in the evening I returned from Pasajes (where I had been on detachment) much fatigued, when orders were issued to take the position in front on the following morning. From the sketch I sent you,[1] you will see their principal force was on the main road at the top of a hill & on a higher hill to the right of it. They had made trenches & batteries in every place likely to be of use. I learned from prisoners that they had 6 regiments, 2 of them light [infantry], with 2 battalions each, in all 8 battalions, between 4 or 5,000 strong. You may see that had they fought as French troops *have* fought, & as they *ought* to have fought, we should have lost a great number if not have been repulsed.

The morning was very heavy but it cleared up & was a fine day. Previous to the business most of our officers laid their account for having 4 or 5 officers & 200 men of the regiment at least knocked over. I longed to have some of you here, you might have seen it all without risk. Nothing could have been fairer than our movements. The division moved down to Vera at day light & stayed there near two hours. The enemy, seeing every man of us move, sent down their light troops to fill the trenches & forts & a small body attempted to defend the first hill with their skirmishers in front a little way down.

The plan was for our brigade to go up the valley between the two main enemy forces. The 2nd brigade more to our left to take the

---

[1] See Letter XXII.

highest hill. Longa (the guerrilla) between us, the regiments of
[?Reina] & El Principe & our pickets on our right. The pickets to
clear the first hill & go round it.

A company of the 95th opened the business. About 20 men with
20 supporting them marched coolly up the hill . . . (Note: If you
remember I told you we never had fought without having rain &
lightning the night before) tho' we had not had any for a month or
6 weeks before & it was a fine day, yet the orders were scarcely
issued before a single cloud came over & we had 10 or 12 flashes
accompanied with loud claps of thunder. The French, who delight in
a long shot (the Spaniards & they are well matched at this – famous
ammunition wasters), began directly they, our men, showed their
heads. However, the 95th moved regularly (I do not mean in a line)
up the hill to within 30 yards of the top without firing & then, by
way of breathing, gave a volley, loaded & advanced to the top, the
support close behind them. The French did not attempt to defend it
but moved to their left, not without music, in quick time. I firmly
believe there are no better troops in the world than the 95th. They
take things so coolly & deliberately & seem to know their business
so well. You have no idea with what glee we saw them & how
readily we fell in to advance as soon as our pickets had cleared the
first hill, which they did soon, tho' it is said by many officers that
there scarcely ever was a stronger position attacked. So well were
the arrangements made that our regiment was under cover almost all
up to the position. The 95th, with one company of ours thrown out to
skirmish, and the pickets, flanked all their trenches & made them run
in all directions so that we marched nearly straight up this hill,
$1\frac{1}{2}$ miles from Vera, in a little more than an hour. The other brigade
had not the advantage of ravines & had to charge several trenches &
forts, which they did most gallantly & this accounts for their loss
being greater than ours.[1]

---

[1] This action, the storming of the heights of Vera, was part of the action
usually known as the crossing of the Bidassoa (7 October). The Light
Division advanced up two spurs with half of Longa's Galician division, about
2,000 men, between them in the re-entrant. It is generally agreed that the
French fought poorly on this day and Soult did not reach the scene of the
fighting, having been misled by Wellington's demonstrations at the extreme
eastern end of the French line. The Light Division succeeded in taking their
objectives with only 370 casualties of which only 3 killed and 16 wounded
fell in the Forty Third.

It was very interesting for us to examine all the works &c. which we had been looking at through glasses for two months. The Spaniards on our right behaved admirably. The hill [La Grande Rhune] they had to attack is at least twice as high as most here & on top of it perpendicular rock with the ruins of a chapel. It is the highest of any near here, not excepting the Crown mountain.[1] They lost many men under it & did not take it for two days. On the 7th Division moving round it they (the French) evacuated it in the night, leaving us in possession of all the Pyrenees. We can now go on any hill we please, not only 'proudly survey them', but send our bâtmen, with covering party, for corn.

There has been a heavy fire from 2 o'clock till nearly this time, 11 o'clock. I hear they have attacked the Spaniards on our right. The 1st & 5th Divisions & Lord Aylmer's brigade are in the valley below us.[2]

The French are hard at work making their extended position as strong as they can. It is generally thought we shall make a general attack. How far we shall go is uncertain. It will be a glorious battle. What a pity we shall have no John Bulls to see it. From these mountains you may see everything that takes place to Bayonne. St Jean de Luz is a beautiful town about a league from the bottom of the mountains, with a river [Nivelle] running through it & a small harbour. There are innumerable single houses all round the country which seems beautiful.

When at Pasajes I went to see the ruins of San Sebastian. It was one of the most beautiful places in Spain. All the houses were large & high, built of free stone with iron balconies. Part of the walls are left with the balconies hanging down. Pasajes is very like Portsmouth, the harbour now full of transports.[3]

---

[1] La Grande Rhune is 900 metres high. The Crown Mountain (Monteaya) on the Spanish bank of the Bidassoa is 826 metres. The French had eight battalions on and around the Rhune and it is hardly surprising that General Giron's 7,000 men of the Army of Reserve of Andalusia failed to seize it although Wellington wrote that they attacked 'in as good order and with as much spirit as I have seen made by any troops'.

[2] The troops he mentioned were on the French bank of the estuary of the Bidassoa.

[3] Pasajes was the main supply port for the army. William Napier described it 'the most romantic beautiful place I almost ever saw – a long

October 17th. The firing I mentioned was caused by the French taking back a hill with a fort on it, 2 hours before daylight. They took 2 companies of Spaniards prisoner.[1] It was in France. As Lord Wellington did not send any English troops, I suppose he did not care for it.

The following questions & answers have passed between the Governor of Pamplona & Don Carlos [de España] :

Q. Will you allow us to march out with baggage into France?

A. No.

Q. If you do not the inhabitants will starve.

A. If I find any one inhabitant dies for want of food while a French soldier has rations, I will slay the Governor.

Q. We will surrender if you will not send us to England but have a Spanish guard.

A. If you want a Spanish guard over you you can have it, & cannot be in a better place.[2]

So that it is likely to surrender soon & I hear the pontoons are gone round to Roncesvalles as the attack is to be on their left. I have just come off picket on the mountain & it has been the worst I have had in this country. The Spanish troops have a longing desire to advance into France. It will require all Lord Wellington's management to prevent their murdering the inhabitants. Plundering I am

---

narrow arm of the sea, for four or five miles between very high and nearly perpendicular rocks surmounted by evergreens, and these again overtopped by the Pyrenees'. (Biography, p. 141. Letter of 19 August 1813.) The sailors were less enamoured of its merits as a harbour.

[1] On the night of 12/13 October the French surprised the Ste. Barbe redoubt three miles east of La Grande Rhune. Larpent noted that 'The day before this surprise the officers at [Fourth Division HQ] were remarking that it was surprising the Spaniards kept the redoubt for the officers were never seen there with their men to keep them on the alert, and the men were cooking without their arms within twenty yards of the French sentries quite unconcerned.' (Larpent *op. cit.*, 277.)

[2] The governor of Pamplona did not open negotiations with General Carlos de España, commanding the investing forces until 25 October, more than a week after this letter was written. When told that surrender as prisoners of war were the only terms that would be accepted, the governor threatened to destroy the city. The reply, made on Wellington's orders, was that if this was done all the officers and n.c.o.s and one private soldier in ten of the garrison would be shot. The garrison surrendered as prisoners of war on 31 October.

The storming of San Sebastian on 31 August 1813, painted by William Heath (*Regimental Museum, The Royal Green Jackets*)

Arcangues church, defended by the 43rd at the battle of the Nive,
viewed from the north (*photograph in the Regimental Museum, The
Royal Green Jackets*)

Wellington and his staff at the battle of the Nivelle
(*National Army Museum*)

sure he cannot. I was on picket the day after the action. A young French soldier was mortally wounded in the side in running down the hill & although he was dying they stripped him entirely naked & left him on the long grass, wet with the evening dew. Our picket found him & told me. When I arrived he was just dead. The Spaniards abuse the French prisoners & the French them, telling them that if it had not been for the redcoats they would have thrashed millions of them. The French officers bear amputations much better than the English. One of our soldiers showed a French prisoner a French major wounded. 'Ah, & the devil go with him,' said the Frenchman, 'for he wanted us to charge you & we knew better.' Some French prisoners in the rear were rejoicing in losing a leg or arm, saying they should now go home & have no more soldiering.

The weather is now always raining or blowing excessively hard. I bought a little pony from one of Longa's sweet youths the other day for 13 dollars.

25th October. It is expected we shall attack in 3 or 4 days.

YOURS &c.
G.H.

8 The Invasion of France

Having captured the high ground on the frontier in his October attack, Wellington was ready to invade France as soon as Pamplona surrendered at the end of the month. He planned to advance on 8 November but heavy rain, swelling the mountain streams, forced a two-day postponement. On this occasion he persuaded Soult that the attack would come at the seaward end of the front and the French were quite unprepared when, instead, Wellington swung forward his inland wing while simultaneously the Light Division struck from the La Rhune massif, breaking the hinge of the door which Hill, on the allied right, was pushing open. By nightfall the allies were in St. Jean de Luz and the French had lost 4,444 men and 69 guns. It was, in Wellington's opinion, 'my best work' and simultaneously news arrived of Napoleon's shattering defeat at Leipzig in the middle of the previous month.

In the upshot the Spaniards plundered so badly that they had to be sent back to their own country but the Anglo-Portuguese army was left firmly established in a triangle of French territory with Bayonne firmly held against them at the apex and with their left on the sea and their right on the river Nive. Both sides had about 63,000 infantry available and no opportunity to employ their cavalry. In these circumstances Wellington was faced with having to divide his army with his opponent having a secure way, through Bayonne, of bringing superior forces against either part.

After another pause for bad weather, the operation began on 9 December when Wellington put four divisions (Second, Third, Sixth and Portuguese) across the Nive while the rest of the army demonstrated towards Bayonne before falling back to their original positions. These, in the case of the Light Division, were around the château and church of Arcangues with their outposts about three-quarters of a mile forward on the ridge around Bassussary. Next day Soult attacked on the west bank with eight divisions against little more than three. Despite some flurry in the first moments, the Light Division had little difficulty in holding Arcangues but on their left there was a crisis. Sir John Hope had put his reserves into billets too far back from the battlefield near Biarritz and it was only with the greatest difficulty and 1,500 casualties that the left flank managed to hold on until the reserves arrived to stabilize the front. The Light Division's fight had cost only 224 men.

There was little fighting on the 11th and 12th but on 13th Soult made his last attack and hurled a three to one superiority of infantry against Hill's 14,000 men on the heights of St. Pierre d'Irube on the east bank of the Nive. His reserves had been withdrawn to strengthen the west bank and floods washed away the pontoons which had been built to enable them to return. By the time they came back by a long detour Hill had won one of the most hard-fought of all the peninsular battles, losing 1,784 men. Soult, however, had shot his bolt and was never again able to launch an attack. All that Wellington had to do was to wait until the weather made the roads passable before invading France in earnest.

LETTER XXV

DEAR BROTHERS,

The day after sending off my last [missing],[1] the left wing of our regiment was for picket 1½ mile in advance. Two companies & a half halted at a handsome house and the other 2½ moved on a mile farther to relieve the pickets in front. Since the 18th we have had very fine weather. Our sentries were sufficiently near to talk to each other. The country here is very hilly. I had *The Times* with me & was reading it. I thought they [the French] might like to see both sides of the question so held up the paper walking down to the ditch that divided us. The vidette[2] immediately walked his horse down & met me. I asked him how he did. He said 'Very well'. I gave him the paper & came away wishing him 'Good morning'. The picket got round him (The paper was the 8th Nov., Genl. Stewart's dispatch)[3]

---

[1] It is particularly unfortunate that Hennell's letter of mid-November has not survived since it would have covered not only his promotion to lieutenant 'vice O'Connell, killed in action', which was dated 22 October although the Gazette carrying the announcement would not have reached the regiment until the first or second week in November, but also the battle of the Nivelle (10 November) in which he was returned as wounded. The wound cannot have been very serious since he was on duty (and makes no reference to its effects) two weeks later. In it the Forty Third played a distinguished role by storming the height known as La Petite Rhune (although according to modern maps it was Mont Alchangue, the feature now shown as Petite Rhune being already in British hands). The cost of this remarkable exploit was four officers and nine rank and file killed and seven officers and fifty rank and file wounded.

[2] A vidette was a mounted sentry or a cavalry outpost, the equivalent of a piquet in the infantry.

[3] Major General the Hon. Sir Charles Stewart was Military Commissioner with the Prussian army in eastern Germany. His despatch brought news of Napoleon's disastrous defeat at Leipzig on 16–18 October.

& sent it to their officer. In $\frac{1}{2}$ an hour an officer and 6 hussars came down to relieve. The officer got off his horse & came down towards us. I immediately met him at the ditch & he came over it without hesitation. We were very polite to each other. He came with me up my hill & asked me if I spoke French. I told him 'no' but that I would send an officer who could. [Captain Samuel] Hobkirk came with two other officers &, on 2 more coming with blue great coats, he asked if they were Portuguese. He stopped talking with us $\frac{3}{4}$ of an hour, saying it was a pity that we were fighting as they esteemed us much as soldiers. I then walked back with him to the ditch & shook hands with him, wishing him 'good day', little suspecting we were so near meeting again, as Hobkirk in all probability did 2 days after. He was the chief of a squadron 10th Hussars, dressed very handsome. He seemed a shrewd man.

Hobkirk & [Lieut. Mackay Hugh] Baillie relieved us next day & we went back to the large house. The owner is a very handsome man about 25 years old. His friends live in Bayonne. He talks to us without any reserve & is very intelligent. He says the inhabitants are very much less annoyed with us than they were with the French.[1] He confirms all that is said about spies watching political conversations. He says persons of the highest nobility down to the shoeblack, are [so] employed as acquaintances, as servants, &c., &c.

Yesterday Soult allowed the inhabitants to return from Bayonne to St. Jean de Luz. The road was covered all day. The Frenchman before mentioned says the people at Bayonne see the falsity of Buonaparte's accounts of the battles in Spain, as, for instance, 'the road to Bayonne was crowded with English prisoners' when not one was seen at the time, but he says they believe what he [Buonaparte] tells them of the north &, altho' the people of the north know what he says of them is false, yet they believe what he says of the south.

Next morning at daylight, instead of coming to relieve us, the brigade came to drive the French back. Of course the picket led the

---

[1] The Marquis d'Arcangues, around whose château the Light Division was to be stationed from mid-November to mid-February, was like most of the people of southwestern France strongly anti-Bonapartist and pro-Bourbon. His report of the feelings of the neighbourhood are borne out from other sources. Wellington wrote a few weeks later 'What do you think of the French people running into our posts for protection from the French troops, with their bundles on their heads and their beds?' (*Correspondence of Lord Burghersh*, p. 55.)

way. We marched under cover of our range of hills in advance. Capt. Hobkirk & Lieut. Baillie with their company & ours (Capt. [Robert] Simpson's) formed in the village opposite to the French pickets &, when the firing commenced on our left, Capt. Hobkirk's company got through the hedge, extended in skirmishing order, & moved on. I was immediately ordered with a section (14 men) to move on his right with orders to put them (the enemy) off the first two hills & halt at a house pointed out.

The whole country is here crowded with small woods, hedges, ditches & houses. As we came upon the first hill the French were running in a crowd upon the 2nd. I opened a fine fire upon them as they went over the hill. We ran down the hollow & then moved up the next & put them off that. I then had as fine a fire upon them as I possibly could have. We were upon a hill & in a ditch up to our shoulders & they were crowding into a narrow pass to get into a wood leading to their support close by in a house, strongly entrenched, behind which they had 9,000 troops & the trenches quite filled with men. I had this fire upon the men in the gateway about $\frac{3}{4}$ of an hour at 300 yards' distance.[1]

I then moved on (the trenched house to my right now) a few yards farther where I found Hobkirk's and [Capt. Thomas] Champ's companies formed with General Kempt. I believe we had now accomplished all we wanted. General Kempt ordered us to move forward. I, being nearest the gap, moved first. He called me back & said 'Now mind, you are not to go beyond the wood.' We were now about 400 yards from their trenches. The 1st 100 yards was a close, the next a thick wood, the two next closes with a slight hedge between them with scarcely any bank or ditch to it.

Just as I came to the edge of the wood, Lieut. Baillie following me at the head of Capt. Hobkirk's company, said 'Here is cavalry! Form up!' I turned round & saw them, & infantry with them much stronger than we, entering the wood on the other side. We formed & gave them such a fire as quickly sent them off. We then moved to the

---

[1] At 300 yards the fire cannot have been very effective. As a contemporary observed, 'a soldier must be very unfortunate indeed who shall be wounded by a common musket at 150 yards, provided that his antagonist aims at him; and as to firing at a man at 200 yards, you may as well fire at the moon.' (Col. George Hanger, 'To all Sportsmen' (1814).) The effective range of a musket was about 80 yards although a lucky shot could kill at much further.

front of the wood, each man to his tree, & kept up a fire upon their trenches. They did not forget to return it but they did little mischief as we were all covered by the trees. The boughs dropped fast around us & the leaves were knocked up by our sides.

After being here ¼ an hour, the *Advance* was sounded (I learned afterwards by mistake). Hobkirk & Baillie moved out of the wood at the head of their men & I at the head of mine, under a tremendous fire, to the slight hedge not more than 90 or 100 yards from their trenches, in which there were at least 2,000 men on the 3 sides. As Baillie came up to the hedge he, with 3 others, was knocked over. Baillie was struck in the forehead & instantly died. I was at the hedge first of my men & instantly laid down flat. Every man got as good a place as he could. The hedge & ditch afforded scarcely any cover. I ordered them to cease firing as for every shot we gave them they sent 5 or 6 in return, all striking within a foot or two of he that fired. At this time our other 4 companies kept a fire upon them. I thought they were going to storm the trenches.

I lay here full an hour, having many wounded round me when, seeing no reserve coming up & our fire slackening much (just at this time 5 of us were lying together; at one time 3 of us were struck, one of them had the bottom of his chin knocked off within a few inches of my face, another was hit in the body & the third in the arm. This determined me to shift my quarters) I desired all around me to crawl on their bodies (If we had crawled on our hands & knees, we shd. all have been knocked over) to our right into the hollow more under cover. I collected in all about 20 men as I went along. As we began crawling a man was killed just by me. When we had got 30 or 40 yards we were under cover & I stayed there about 20 minutes, setting a man to watch if they came out of their trenches, pointing out the road to retire by.

The *Retire* sounded. They [the French] immediately rushed out of their trenches & I made the best of my way with my men over a little hill behind a hedge under a tremendous fire to some houses in rear on a hill, where I found 2 companies. After leaving 18 men under the command of Lieut. [Lawrence] Steel, we retired to the rest of the regiment. Before we left the house we learned that Hobkirk with 12 or 14 men were made prisoners. Lieut. Steel was to retire to the position we wanted and then halt. He had a shot in his leg but it is not a bad wound. Thus ended at 2 o'clock p.m. a skirmish which, but for the mistake, would only have cost us 10 men wounded. As it is we have 1 capt. missing, 1 lieut killed, 1 wounded, 2 sergeants, 76 men killed, wounded or missing. Thus I have passed, as you will see, the hottest fire I ever saw, Badajoz not excepted. I was in 10 or 20 times more danger than in either the battles of Salamanca or Vitoria and I have not received the slightest injury. A loud cry of gratitude. It shall not be unattended to. If I live to return, I shall have many remarks of a serious nature it would not be proper to place here.

As I got to the regiment Rutherford [Ensign, 94th Regiment] came to me (the 3rd Division was called out to support us if we required it). He told me Baillie's friends were intimate with the Ballantines of Edinburgh. Baillie was a fine young man [who] had just come out from England with Hobkirk, bringing a most superb kit (viz; clothes, canteens, tent &c.). He is worth, I understand, £700 a year. Hobkirk spends nearly £1,000 a year. A flag of truce was sent to ask permission for his private servant & baggage to go to him, which was granted & I hear today that Lord Wellington has sent the names of 4 French captains for them to choose one in exchange, so he will very likely return. Lord Wellington knows him personally.[1]

---

[1] No reference to Wellington having asked for Hobkirk to be exchanged appears in the Despatches and, if he did ask, he was unsuccessful. Hobkirk spent the rest of the war as a prisoner. The affair in front of Arcangues was quite unnecessary. William Napier, who had been commanding the battalion since the beginning of November when Daniel Hearn went home sick, wrote to his wife on 24 November: 'We had an affair yesterday which has caused me much mortification. We were meant to take possession of a ridge for our outposts, which we did for the loss of less than ten men; but no general that *we* had understood what was wanted, and instead of halting us allowed us to halt ourselves. Some young sanguine officers who are more vain than good, concluded that with three or four companies they could drive the whole French army before them; the result was that I lost 75 men – more than I did in the last action [Nivelle] . . . And I run the risk of being called the cause of the misfortune, as I know that generals are sometimes not very scrupulous in blaming others to save their credit. They have already thrown the whole blame upon these officers who went forward, forgetting that they themselves were the original and principal cause of it, all through ignorance in not knowing where to stop, or pointing out what they had wished to have done.' (Napier *op. cit.*, 162.)

It is clear from Hennell's letter that Napier was wrong in blaming the generals for pushing on too far since Major General Kempt, the brigadier responsible, made it quite clear how far they were to go.

Major Napier called the officers together yesterday delicately to point out to them the necessity of judgment & caution in the field. He said it was not necessary at this time of day for the officers of the 43rd to show themselves men of courage.

By a deserter we learn that the French have 9,000 men on this side of the Nive & 1,000 at Bayonne[1] & that they lost 100 men on the 23rd. Reports are various here we are entrenching the position we now have. We took a great deal of ground on our left by pushing them as we did. There is no reason why we should not advance. I find that if I had remained near Hobkirk I should certainly have been taken prisoner as full 200 men rushed out of the trenches & leaped over the hedge upon him.

27th November 1813. The wet seems setting in again today. I find I am now quite broke into fighting, I was in no fears or flurries on the 23rd. The owner of the large house told us that France had refused to furnish Buonaparte with more conscripts.[2] Lord Wellington & Soult are frequently writing to each other, I suppose only on military matters. There is very little plundering going forward. The very rigorous measures taken has stopped it.[3] We have good forage for our horses. I have only one & shall buy no more. Peace is now I think fairly beyond a doubt & it is likely to be speedy & soon. The half-pay monster is staring some of us lieutenants in the face again. However,

---

[1] Either through ignorance or design the deserter greatly understated the French force available on the west bank of the Nive. Although Soult had moved much of his army to the east bank there were not less than 25,000 infantry between Wellington's outposts and Bayonne, which had a garrison of more than 8,000.

[2] To build yet another *Grande Armée* after the defeat at Leipzig, Napoleon called up the classes of 1814 and 1815. These, together with the cancellations of many hitherto exempt and the mobilization of such bodies as customs officers and *gardes forestiers*, should have given him 1,000,000 men but less than a quarter of this number became available and the wooded parts of France were plagued with bands of young evaders.

[3] There was a violent outbreak of looting when the army fought its way into occupied villages in France after the battle of the Nivelle. The Spaniards were the chief offenders but three or four British and Portuguese soldiers, caught plundering by the Provost Marshal, were hanged on the spot without trial. Wellington, however, was determined that the allied army should not raise against itself the kind of resistance that French looting had raised in Spain and sent all the Spanish troops back to Spain. This sacrificed his numerical superiority but gained him the trust of the French people.

I heartily wish for it. I have seen the dreadful calamities of war & I find soldiers feel much less for themselves than their friends feel for them. I suppose you will feel the good effects of peace in your trades.

If I had been wounded sufficiently for the pension on the 10th November, I should have had the lieut's pension, as I was gazetted on the 9th.[1] If the agent's, Cox & Co., were spoken to I think they would antedate [Benjamin Hutcheon] Edward's commission & mine to the time of Lieuts. Folliet's & O'Connell's deaths. It is frequently done.[2]

I long to receive the trunk & letters. I shall answer most of them soon. It [the trunk] must be stopped at Santander. I have written to a corporal of ours there, so I shall probably have it soon.

4 o'clock. Major Napier has just told me that it is my turn to go home. He will apply for leave for me to join the 2nd Batt. & for many reasons I have accepted it so I shall be in London at Xmas, when I shall state my reasons & am quite sure you will fully agree with me. I shall get the trunk & sell the contents & bring home as many guineas as I can. Major Napier tells me we may expect no more fighting.[3]

---

[1] His promotion was dated 22 October but appeared in the Gazette of 9 November. A lieutenant's pension for the loss of an eye or a limb in action would have been £70 a year, compared to an ensign's pension of £50. This was in addition to his pay or half pay. The loss of either an eye or a limb was not necessarily cause for an officer to stop regimental service. Edward Freer of the Forty Third had lost his right arm at Badajoz in 1812 and continued on full pay until 1817. Major Matthew Sutton, Ninety Seventh, continued to serve until he retired in May 1814 although he had been totally blind since August 1810.

[2] The delay of more than seven weeks between O'Connell's death and Hennell's appointment to his vacancy was unusually long. Three to four weeks was the normal time but antedating to the actual time of the vacancy occurring was extremely rare although Lieutenant and Captain M. J. Wynyard, Second Guards, managed to get his promotion redated to his predecessor's death in 1809.

[3] On the same day as this letter was written Napier wrote to his wife: 'I trust a peace will soon put an end to all your anxiety.' Unfortunately he underestimated Napoleon's willingness to make peace on terms acceptable to his enemies. He rejected the Frankfurt proposals, put to him on 6 November, which would have left him with France's 'natural frontiers', with his eastern border on the Rhine. This proposal, leaving him in possession of Antwerp, was unacceptable to Britain and no future offer included more than France's 'Ancient Limits'.

Remember me to all my friends & tell them I hope to meet them in great good spirits & none more so than you,

Your affectionate brother,
George Hennell.

LETTER XXVI

Cantonments near Arbonne. 1½ leagues from Bayonne.
15th Dec. 1813.

DEAR BROTHERS,

Instead of London, I shall most likely eat my Xmas dinner here. Lord Wellington will grant no leaves of absence now. I will now state my principal reasons for intending to come home. As our 1st batt. is only 650 or 700 strong [and] the 2nd batt. only about 200, the oldest & most experienced officers say that there is no doubt that, in case of a peace, the officers of the 2nd batt. would have to go on half-pay & it was thought by most [that] I might get an exchange into another regiment for £100 or £150 or I might get into a single batt. regiment & then I should not go on half-pay.[1] There are some other powerful reasons why an exchange would be desirable. If we go home the principal is that in England we should be obliged to live at great expense. Think over the exchange &, if you approve of it, go to Greenwood & Cox & see who wish to get into the 43rd & leave your address to receive proposals for an exchange, advising me of what you are doing.[2]

---

[1] The assumption was that when the war ended the army would be reduced to its pre-war strength – seventy seven regiments of infantry of the line of which only two, the First and Sixtieth, had more than one battalion. Twenty two of the seventy seven old regiments still had only one battalion in 1813 (two of these raised second battalions in 1814) and the officers of these were considered as certain to be continued on full-pay after the peace as were the officers of the first battalion of the remaining fifty five old regiments. Hennell, although serving with 1st battalion Forty Third, was properly on the strength of the 2nd battalion since his promotion.

[2] With the consent of their colonels, any two officers of equal regimental rank could exchange regiments. It was not uncommon for the officer wishing to exchange to pay the other to move to another regiment. This was certainly connived at by the authorities although both parties would have to

I shall now give you an account of what I saw of the 5 days' fighting. On the 8th we had orders to be under arms 2 hours before daylight & at that time we marched to our pickets. About 8 o'clock the 5th & 1st Divisions commenced a sharp skirmish just over the hill in front of us, to our left. The firing becoming heavier every 5 minutes till it was, as Major Napier told us, as pretty a hot skirmish as you would ever wish to see & as hard fighting. This continued $1\frac{1}{2}$ hours & then slackened but continued till near night, when General Hope was within reach nearly of the guns at Bayonne on our left. Our regiment & the 95th had to give the outlying pickets & supports.

That night our company was the most on the right on picket, within shot of the entrenched house mentioned in my last in possession of the French. They had placed their pickets at a house about 100 yards in front of us. Ours were upon the edge of a hill in a house. In relieving they fired at every man who showed his nose on either side of the house.[1] It was wet till 9 o'clock, then fine moonlight. We [heard] the 2nd, 3rd & 6th Divisions fighting over the river till past dark.

At 12 o'clock the field officer [of the day] came & ordered us to withdraw the picket without making the slightest noise, the sentries also by degrees, so that it might not be perceived, to a hill half a mile more in rear. All the pickets were so withdrawn. We did not know the reason, we now know it well. The 1st Division retired that night & the 5th also part of the way.[2]

As soon as we could see we perceived troops moving very fast

---

sign a declaration that 'upon my word as an officer and a gentleman I will not, either now or at any future time, give or receive, by any means or in any shape whatever, directly or indirectly, any consideration'. The colonel would also have to give his statement that 'I verily believe no clandestine bargain subsists between the parties concerned'.

[1] This was most unusual. Between the French and the British it was an unwritten law that the advanced posts should not molest each other. If one army intended to advance they would signify to the opposing piquets that they should get out of the way. Wellington remarked, 'I always encouraged this; the killing of a poor fellow of a vidette or carrying off a post could not influence the battle, and I always when I was going to attack sent to tell them to get out of the way.'

[2] The First Division had withdrawn seven miles to St. Jean de Luz and the Fifth went back three miles leaving the front line to two Portuguese brigades.

from behind the entrenched house to our left in great numbers before we moved. The French are very fond of sneaking by twos & threes into a wood or house & there forming for an attack. However, there was no 2 or 3 here for Soult had brought all his disposable force, except one corps to [guard against] Hill & keep Bayonne, to attack our left. The [French] sharpshooters had no knapsacks on to give our pickets a good chase, which they did in quick time. It was a very fine hunt. Our company was not pushed but some on our left were.[1] The French were on one side of the hedge & ours on the other. One of our officers found himself & men on the wrong side. On discovering it he said, 'Come, my lads, charge!' They jumped over & soon cleared their way through them, not without some music.[2]

On arriving at the large house mentioned in my last. There is a church to the left of it with a wood in front. The trees being cut half through & broken down make a very strong place as the château & church were entrenched & loopholed. This was our position & an excellent one it is. The 95th & most of our company had formed behind the wall in front. We were moving to the left a few yards when the enemy appeared on a hill opposite, about 200 yards off. We ought to have waited till they came into the wood before us but the moment our soldiers saw them in some numbers they all at once opened one of the most tremendous fires I, & many older than myself, ever beheld. I have since been to the house & trees round it, where the French appeared, & there is scarcely one tree without 20 balls stuck in it. They got behind hedges & ditches, threw up trenches & opened a two, a four and a six pounder upon the church which it struck 6 or 8 times but did us no harm.

Soon after this Soult attacked Hope in a most determined manner with at least 40,000 men. The 5th Division bore the brunt of it &

---

[1] John Cooke wrote that 'At half past nine a.m., the enemy's skirmishers came forward in a careless fashion, talking to each other, and good naturedly allowed our sentinels to retire without firing at them.' He says that previously they had called out to them 'to retire' in French and Spanish. (Cooke *op. cit.*, ii 60.) It was on Hennell's right, not his left, that the heaviest pressure came and an officer and thirty men of the Rifles were captured.

[2] Lieutenant Duncan Campbell (called Cameron in the regimental history) found the French in a hollow road between himself and his own regiment. Calling his men to him, he led them, sword in hand, through the enemy and escaped with about ninety men.

maintained their position. The 1st [Division] & Lord Aylmer's brigade supported it.[1]

During this our 2nd brigade had some skirmishes with them about ½ a mile to our left. We began strengthening our church & next morning (11th), a fine day, began to make a battery for 9 guns in front of the church. They [the French] began again on the left. Genl. Hope was about a mile & a half from us, between us & the sea & near the high road. We were supported by the 4th Division close up. The 7th [Division] came up which made them suppose we intended to attack them in the centre. They formed their columns & threw out their skirmishers which made us expect an attack from them. We were soon at our posts & had orders to defend it to the last &, if they came up a lane to our left, to charge them down it again.

About this time Douro, Lord Wellington, came to the church to reconnoitre. He said in the room, 'I don't care what they do here,' & in a minute, after looking through his glass, 'Hallo, they are going to attack Hope again, I'll be off.' He went back again & we all thought Douro out for once, for all was quiet till 4 o'clock & as we were saying 'Douro, my lad, you are out', a cannon gave the signal & in one minute both the French & our lines opened on the old ground on the left a tremendous fire which lasted till dark. Our battery was getting very forward. We had working parties all night & it was finished by daylight.

It is reported by deserters that we were to be attacked by 80 picked companies. I saw the Dutchmen[2] form on the night they deserted. Their plan was well laid. A man was to hide himself while skirmishing & come in to tell us that 2 officers would come in at night to form a plan & make their proposal, viz : to be

---

[1] The Fifth Division were retiring before the reinforcements arrived. Gleig, a subaltern in the Eighty Fifth (Aylmer's brigade) wrote 'Our people were giving way. But no sooner had the head of our column shown itself than their confidence completely returned and they renewed their struggle with increased alacrity.' (Gleig *op. cit.*, 172.)

[2] On 12 December Wellington reported to London: 'I have the pleasure to inform you that after the affair with the enemy on the 10th instant, two battalions of the regiment of Nassau and one of the Francfort regiment, under the command of Colonel Kruse, passed over to the allied army, on the condition that they should be sent to Germany.' (WD xi 360.) It was not uncommon in English at this time to refer to Germans as Dutch (Deutsch).

conveyed immediately to Holland. All was agreed. They threw out a picket & sentries towards the French & the colonel led them in without a shot being fired. There were 2 regiments of Nassau & one of Frankfurt, about 1,500 strong. Another regiment wished to desert but the colonel was wounded. Next day 45 deserted to our division & as many more last night. It is said Soult has sent all Dutch & Germans prisoner to the rear.

During the time they were fighting on the left & within $\frac{1}{2}$ a mile of us (there being no firing with us) the French came, 20 together, walking about the field in front of us, and our men standing on the wall all afternoon. While another officer & myself were standing on the wall, we saw some of our men getting through the wood and run[ning] into a house to fill their havresacks with apples. They went without their firelocks. We thought we saw some blue coats as well as red. The fact was the French were going as fast as our men into the same room. They too left their firelocks behind. At one time there were 17 Frenchmen & as many of ours at the same heap of apples. There were some of the French 43rd regiment & they looked at our fellows' breastplates & took hold of their hands & shook them. They were so glad to see them, gave them some brandy & said if they would come up to the house with them they would give them a canteen full & asked about each others' rations. Our fellows said they had plenty of rations, sometimes double. The French told them *they* had plenty of brandy but only $\frac{1}{2}$ lb of bread & $\frac{3}{4}$ lb of meat & that not regular. If our fellows had gone to the camp with them for brandy, I daresay they would have given it to them & suffered them to come back. One of our men heard a person behind him say, "Damn your eyes, stand off those apples' & on turning round was surprised to see a Frenchman. All foreigners learn to swear in English first.

As soon as Major Napier knew of it he sent an officer, a sergeant & 3 men with arms to bring our men prisoners away. He met a Frenchman coming out. The fellow stared. He told him to run off. '*Oui, oui, monsieur*', he replied & walked off. The French never offered to fire on them, though they saw what they were coming for. Thus did men who, a few hours before, were firing at & endeavouring to bayonet each other make as good friends as Englishmen in a pot house.

Next morning (13th) we found Soult had begun moving his troops at 10 o'clock at night to attack with all his force Hill on the other side [of] the Nive. Douro was aware of him. At 11 o'clock at night 2 bridges were formed across the Nive &, by the time they were needed, the 3rd, 6th, 4th & 7th Divisions were up in support.[1] We saw the firing & you will know as much as I shall. Douro said to General Kempt in passing us at 4 o'clock in the afternoon in high spirits, 'I have often seen the French licked but I never knew them get such a hell of a licking as Hill has given them.' We heard there were 15,000 dead on the field & many with bayonet wounds. To every one killed we reckon 4 wounded.[2] The Portuguese behaved admirably; they charged 3 times. It is reported Hill has cut off their communications down the Adour & they receive all their provisions by water carriage as the ground on the other side of the Adour is swampy so that, if they cannot bring them down the other branch, they must retire.

My newspapers have just arrived up to the 29th. I am quite well. We never had our clothes off till last night since 12 o'clock on the 8th. Sergeant Palmer, his wife & child are well & in the same house with me. I long to enjoy the good news with my friends when it is completed. Until then,

> Yours &c.
> G.H.

---

[1] Owing to the bridge across the Nive at Villefranque having been swept away by the flooding river, only one battalion (9th Caçadores) from Sixth Division arrived in time to fire a shot before Hill's force had repulsed Soult's attack. Wellington rode up to Sir Rowland, took his hand and said, 'Hill, the day's your own.'

[2] French casualties on 13 December were about 3,300. The total French casualties for the five days' fighting, 9–13, were about 5,900 killed, wounded and missing. The proportion of killed to wounded in this battle was 1 :9. The proportion in the Anglo-Portuguese army was 1 :4½.

Postscript

The battle of the Nive was the last in which George Hennell took part. Soon after it he was posted home to the 2nd battalion. It is not clear how his wish to return to England was granted since, in his last letter, he was confident that he would not be allowed to do so. It is possible that he was given leave because his Nivelle wound was worse than had been thought but a more likely explanation is that 1st battalion Forty Third was over establishment in lieutenants. A battalion on war service was entitled to two lieutenants to each of its ten companies exclusive of the adjutant should he be a lieutenant. In December 1813 the Forty Third had at least twenty-two lieutenants (including Adjutant Steel) in the field and more were on their way from England. It seems probable, therefore, that Hennell was allowed to join his proper battalion since he was surplus to establishment in southern France. Whatever the reason, his transfer meant that he missed the closing months of the war and the final battle at Toulouse on 10 April 1814. He also missed the regiment's next overseas service when, in October of that year, it sailed to take part in the war against the United States. The Forty Third was one of the few regiments to distinguish itself in the ill-fated attempt to capture New Orleans in January 1815.

By that time Hennell had achieved his wish to get an exchange. On 24 November 1814 he was transferred to the Thirty Ninth (Dorsetshire) Foot, Lieutenant Samuel Curtis of that regiment taking his place in the Forty Third. The exchange, however, did not achieve his ambition of staying on full pay after the peace. The Thirty Ninth was also a two-battalion regiment and, since Hennell despite his army seniority would have joined it as junior lieutenant, he would have been posted to the 2nd battalion. This, once the alarms of the Hundred Days were past, was disbanded and on 25 February 1816 all the officers were put on half-pay.

Nothing is known of George Hennell after the war except that, at some stage, he married Miss Rosalie Garnier. There were no children of the marriage, which lasted until Hennell's death in July 1831.

Appendix 1

BIOGRAPHICAL NOTES

Aylmer, Maj. Gen. Matthew, 5th Baron (1775–1850). Given command of an independent brigade from July 1813 after service as Deputy Adjutant General in the Peninsula.

Beresford, Marshal William Carr (1768–1854). Natural son of 1st Marquess of Waterford. Commanded Portuguese army 1809–22 (see note 2 on p. 127). Defeated Soult at Albuera, 1811. Wellington considered him his ablest subordinate. Baron 1814, Viscount 1823.

Campbell, Col. James (1773?–1835). Commissioned 1st Foot 1791. Major 94th Foot 1802; Lt. Col. 94th 1804. Served in India 1802–7 and in Peninsula. Severely wounded at Salamanca and at Vitoria.

Carr, Lt. Col. Henry William (1778?–1821). Commissioned 68th Foot 1794. Capt. 83rd Foot 1796; Major 1807. Commanded 2/83rd in Peninsula 1811–14. Bt. Lt. Col. after storm of Badajoz. Subsequently K.C.B. and Equerry to Duke of Kent.

Clausel, Gen. Count Bertrand (1772–1842). Commanded division in Army of Portugal 1810–12 and succeeded to command of that army at Salamanca. Commanded Army of North 1813 and a corps under Soult 1813–14. Subsequently Governor of Algeria and Marshal of France.

Cole, Lt. Gen. Hon. Galbraith Lowry (1772–1842). 2nd son 1st Earl of Enniskillen. Commissioned 1787. Maj. Gen. 1808. Commanded Fourth Division in Peninsula. Subsequently Governor of Mauritius and Cape of Good Hope.

Dalhousie, Lt. Gen. George Ramsay, 9th Earl of (1770–1838). Commissioned 1788. Commanded Seventh Division in Peninsula 1812–14. Subsequently Governor of Canada and G.O.C. India.

De España, Maj. Gen. Carlos (1775–1839). French *emigré* (Charles d'Espagne) who joined Spanish army after French revolution. Governor of Madrid 1812. Murdered in Carlist wars.

Biographical Notes

Gazan, General Count Honoré Théophile Maxime (1765–1845). Commanded Army of the South 1813. Chief of Staff to Soult 1813–14.

Graham, Lt. Gen. Sir Thomas (1748–1843). Raised 90th Foot at own expense 1794. A.D.C. to Sir John Moore in Coruña campaign 1808–9. Lt. Gen. 1810. Defeated Marshal Victor at Barossa 1811. Commanded First Division and left wing of army 1811–13 when went home sick. Created Lord Lyndoch 1814. Founded United Service Club.

Hill, Lt. Gen. Sir Rowland (1772–1842). Commissioned 1790. Commanded Second Division 1809–14 and right wing of army 1813–14. Created Baron 1814, Viscount 1842. Commander in Chief of British army 1828–39.

Hope, Lt. Gen. Sir John (1765–1823). 2nd son 2nd Earl of Hopetoun. Commissioned 1784. Succeeded Graham as commander left wing of Peninsular army in 1813. Created Baron Niddry 1814. Succeeded as 4th Earl of Hopetoun 1816.

Joseph, King of Spain (1768–1844). Born Count Giuseppe Buonaparte, elder brother of Napoleon. Appointed King of Naples 1806 and transferred to Spain 1808. Rusticated to his French estate after defeat at Vitoria. Fled to U.S.A. after Waterloo. Died in Florence.

Jourdan, Marshal Jean Baptiste (1762–1833). Served with French army in American War of Independence. Divisional commander in 1793. Led Army of Sambre and Meuse to victory of Fleurus 1794. Marshal of the Empire 1804. Chief of Staff to King Joseph in 1809 and 1812–13.

Kempt, Maj. Gen. James (1764–1854). Commissioned 1783. Maj. Gen. 1811. Commanded brigade in Third Division 1811–13, in Light Division 1813–14 and at Waterloo. Subsequently Governor of Nova Scotia and Canada.

Longa, Maj. Gen. Francisco. Gunsmith from Rioja who became a guerrilla leader in 1808. Gazetted colonel in Spanish army 1812; Maj. Gen. 1813.

March, Capt. Charles Lennox, Earl of (1791–1860). Eldest son 4th Duke of Richmond. As Captain 52nd L.I. was A.D.C. to Wellington through most of Peninsular campaigns. Succeeded as 5th Duke 1819.

Marmont, Marshal August Frédéric Louis de, Duke of Ragusa (1774–1852). Horse artillery officer who became A.D.C. to Bonaparte. Commanded Army of Portugal May 1811 until severely wounded at Salamanca. Temporarily disgraced but restored to play leading part in Paris campaign of 1814.

Mina, Francisco Epoz y (1784–1836). A Navarrese who became the greatest and most effective of the Spanish guerrilla leaders, at one time levying customs duty on the French army's supplies crossing into Spain. Made a regular major general in 1813. Later fought for the Carlists.

Morillo, Maj. Gen. Pablo (1777–1838). Lieutenant in Spanish army 1809 who rose to command Galician division in 1813. His men were the best disciplined in Spanish army.

Napier, Lt. Col. William Francis Patrick (1785–1860). Commissioned 1800. Captain 43rd Foot 1804. Commanded 1st battalion 43rd at Salamanca, Nivelle and Nive. Published *History of the War in the Peninsula and the South of France* 1828–40.

Orange, Lt. Col. William, Hereditary Prince of (1782–1849). A.D.C. to Wellington 1811–13. Briefly engaged to Princess Charlotte of Wales and promoted British general 1814. Commanded corps in Waterloo campaign. Succeeded as King William II of the Netherlands.

Phillipon, Gen. Baron Armand (1761–1836). Promoted from ranks of Bourbon Regiment of Lorraine. Brigade commander at Eylau. Governor of Badajoz. After capture there escaped from England only to be captured again at Battle of Külm, August 1813.

Picton, Lt. Gen. Sir Thomas (1758–1815). Commissioned 1772. Maj. Gen. 1808. Commanded Third Division 1810–12 and 1813–14. Killed at Waterloo.

Ross, Lt. Col. Hew Dalrymple (1779–1868). Commissioned R.A. 1795. Commanded A (the Chestnut) Troop, Royal Horse Artillery, in Peninsula 1809–14 and at Waterloo. Brevet Lt. Col. 1813; Field Marshal 1868.

Sanchez, Maj. Gen. Don Julian. Retired regular soldier who raised mounted guerrilla in Leon and New Castille. Cooperated closely with Wellington around Ciudad Rodrigo. His guerrilla converted into two regular cavalry regiments in 1813.

Somerset, Lt. Col. Lord Fitzroy (1788–1855). 7th son 5th Duke of Beaufort. As captain 43rd L.I. was A.D.C. to Wellington 1808–10 and subsequently his Military Secretary. As Field Marshal Lord Raglan commanded British army in the Crimea 1854–55.

Souham, Gen. Joseph (1760–1837). Promoted from ranks of Bourbon Cuirassiers. Commanded Army of Portugal in late 1812. Later severely wounded at Battle of Leipzig.

Soult, Marshal Nicholas Jean-de-Dieu, Duke of Dalmatia (1769–1851). In ranks of Bourbon army. Second in command to Massena in defence of Switzerland and Genoa. Distinguished at Austerlitz. Commanded corps in Spain 1808–9, Army of the South 1810–12, Army of Spain 1813–14. Chief of Napoleon's staff at Waterloo. Minister of War under Louis Philippe.

Stewart, Lt. Gen. Sir Charles (1778–1854). Half-brother to Lord Castlereagh. Adjutant General in the Peninsula 1809–12. Mission to Prussian army 1813–14. Created Lord Stewart 1814. Succeeded as 3rd Marquess of Londonderry 1822.

Suchet, Marshal Louis Gabriel, Duke of Albufera (1772–1826). Served under Massena at Genoa. Commanded armies on east coast of Spain 1811–14.

Worcester, Lieutenant Henry Somerset, Marquess of (1792–1853). Eldest son 6th Duke of Beaufort. As lieutenant 10th Light Dragoons (Hussars) was A.D.C. to Wellington 1812–14. Succeeded as 7th Duke of Beaufort 1835.

Appendix 2

OFFICERS OF THE FORTY THIRD (MONMOUTHSHIRE) FOOT
(LIGHT INFANTRY)

during the service of George Hennell, June 1812–November 1814

	Regimental Seniority
COLONEL	
Lt. Gen. Sir John Cradock KB	7 Jan 09
Governor of the Cape of Good Hope 1811–14	
Promoted General 4 Jun 14.	
LIEUTENANT COLONELS	
William Giffard (Brevet Colonel 4 Jun 11)	19 Sep 04
Deputy Adjutant General, Malta, 1810–14.	
Promoted Major General 4 Jun 14.	
Daniel James Hearn	14 May 12
Commanded 1st battalion at Vitoria.	
Retired 4 Aug 14.	
MAJORS	
Christopher Patrickson (B/Lt. Col. 30 May 11)	28 Sep 09
Promoted Lieutenant Colonel (supernumerary),	
without purchase, 17 Jun 13.	
Commanded 1st battalion at Toulouse.	
Peter Deshon	16 Aug 10
Exchanged to 85th Foot, 25 Jan 13.	
Joseph Wells	10 Oct 11
Promoted Lieutenant Colonel by purchase	
vice Hearn, 4 Aug 14.	

Officers of the Forty Third Light Infantry

	Regimental Seniority
William Francis Patrick Napier	30 May 11[1]
Lieutenant Colonel by brevet, 22 Nov 13.	14 May 12
Commanded 1st battalion at Salamanca, Nivelle & Nive.	

Nicholas Alexander Mein	21 Sep 09
From 85th Foot by exchange vice Deshon	25 Jan 13
Lieutenant Colonel by brevet 4 Jun 14.	

CAPTAINS

John Duffy (Brevet Major 6 Feb 12)	12 Aug 04
Promoted Major without purchase	
vice Patrickson, 17th Jun 13.	
Robert Dalzell	26 Aug 04
Major by brevet, 12 Apr 14.	
James Fergusson	11 Dec 06
Promoted Major, 79th Foot, by purchase, 3 Feb 13.	
James Watson Hull (or Hall)[2]	11 Jun 07
Retired (receiving £500) 16 Jul 12.	
Saumarez Brock	28 Mar 05
	6 Aug 07
Thomas Lear Strode	25 Dec 12
Retired 25 Jun 12.	
William Haverfield	31 Mar 08
Promoted Major by purchase vice Wells, 11 Aug 14.	
Lord Fitzroy Somerset (Brevet Lieutenant Colonel, 27 Apr 12)	18 Aug 12
Military Secretary & 1st A.D.C. to Lord Wellington.	
Promoted Captain & Lieutenant Colonel, 1st Foot Guards	
without purchase, 25 Jul 14.	
William Sherran	8 Sep 08
Thomas Champ	15 Sep 08

---

[1] Where two dates are shown the first is the officer's seniority in the army (i.e. by brevet promotion or by rank previously held in another regiment). The second date shows regimental seniority on which promotion within the regiment depended. A purchasing officer could not buy over the head of another officer ready to purchase.

[2] Where alternative spellings of surnames are shown these represent the spelling given in the Army List.

Robert P. Murchison	8 Mar 09
Died of wounds at the Nivelle, 10 Nov 13.	
Joseph Chapman	9 Mar 09
John Proctor	4 May 09
Robert Simpson	17 Aug 09
Thomas M'Kenzie	27 Sep 09
Died in Portugal, 3 Dec 12.	
Sir James Maxwell Tylden, Kt. (Brevet Major 19 Dec 11)	28 Sep 09
John Swinburne(e)	15 Aug 10
George Johnston (or Johnson)	16 Aug 10
William Morrison	27 Dec 10
(prisoner of war in France).	
John Paul Hopkins	29 Aug 11
John Pitts	10 Oct 11
Thomas Rylance	14 May 12

LIEUTENANTS

James Shaw (later Shaw Kennedy)	23 Jan 06
A.D.C. to Major General Charles Alten.	
Promoted Captain without purchase vice Hull, 16 Jul 12.	
Samuel Pollock	21 May 06
Promoted Captain without purchase vice M'Kenzie, 18 Feb 13.	
George Ridout	2 Jul 06
Died of wounds at San Muñoz, 23 Nov 12.	
Thomas Capel	11 Dec 06
Promoted Captain without purchase vice Duffy, 1 Jul 13.	
Killed in action at the Nivelle, 10 Nov 13.	
William Freer	5 Feb 07
Promoted Captain without purchase vice Capel, 1 Dec 13.	
Henry Booth	11 Jan 07
Promoted Captain by purchase vice Strode, 25 Jul 12.	
Bernard Murphy (formerly sergeant major)	31 Dec 07
Adjutant, 2nd battalion from 31 Dec 07 until	
Promoted Captain without purchase vice Murchison, 2 Dec 13.	
Samuel Hobkirk	7 Apr 08
Promoted Captain by purchase vice Fergusson, 3 Dec 12.	
John Buchanan	5 May 08
Placed on half-pay, 24 Aug 14.	

Officers of the Forty Third Light Infantry

	Regimental Seniority
Lyons Enright (or Engracht) *Resigned 10 Dec 12[1].*	1 Sep 08
George Houlton	6 Oct 08
Cooke Tylden Pattenson *Promoted Captain by purchase vice Haverfield, 18 Aug 14.*	9 Mar 09
George Berkeley	6 Apr 09
Wyndham Madden	2 May 09
John Campbell Lunn	17 Aug 09
Thomas Lalor	17 Oct 09
Roger Frederick *Promoted without purchase to Captain, 1st Ceylon Regiment, 9 Jul 12.*	18 Oct 09
Richard Brunton *Serving with Portuguese Army as Captain, 6th Cacadores. Promoted without purchase to Captain, 60th Foot, 10 Nov 13.*	12 Dec 09
Charles Mayne *Died in Portugal, January 1813.*	13 Dec 09
John O'Connell *Killed in action at San Sebastian, 31 Aug 13.*	14 Dec 09
Hon. Charles Gore A.D.C. to Major General James Kempt.	4 Jan 10
Thomas Wilkinson *Exchanged to 85th Foot, 25 Jan 13.*	18 Jan 10
John Henry Cooke (or Cook)	19 Apr 10
John Angrove *Died of wounds received at the Nivelle, 13 Nov 13.*	24 May 10
John Montgomery Hill	28 Jun 10
Edward Freer *Killed in action at the Nivelle, 10 Nov 13.*	12 Jul 10
Samuel Phillimore Beavan *Resigned, 2 Sep 10.*	21 Aug 10
Edward D'Arcey	22 Aug 10
John Meyricke	23 Aug 10
James Considine	27 Dec 10
John Maclean	27 Mar 11

---

[1] Officers who had purchased their commissions retired: non-purchase officers resigned.

Appendix 2

	Regimental Seniority
John Gibson Jones	31 Aug 09
	28 Mar 11
Richard Carroll	2 May 11
Philip Macpherson	13 Jun 11
Mackay Hugh Baillie	18 Jul 11
Killed in action near Arcangues, 29 Nov 13.	
Duncan Campbell	29 Aug 11
Henry Bambrick	12 Sep 11
Alexander Steel(e)	7 Nov 11
Richard Whalley	16 Apr 12
Died Feb 13.	
William Havelock	12 May 12
Extra A.D.C. to Major General Charles Alten, 1813–14.	
William Williams	13 May 12
Resigned 3 Mar 14.	
George Folliet	14 May 12
Killed in action near Zalain de Lesaca, 31 Aug 13.	
Bartholomew Casey	21 May 12
George Hood	28 May 12

- -

James Imlach	23 Jul 12
From 85th Foot by exchange vice Wilkinson, 25 Jan 13.	25 Jan 13

- -

ENSIGNS

William Murphy	30 Aug 10
Promoted Lieutenant without purchase vice Bramwell, 4 Jan 12.	
Died 7 Oct 13.	
Robert Craufurd	27 Dec 10
Promoted Lieutenant without purchase vice Booth, 25 Jun 12.	
Benjamin Whichcote	31 Jan 11
Promoted Lieutenant without purchase vice Frederick, 16 Jul 12.	
Thomas Hunt Grubbe	28 Mar 11
Promoted Lieutenant by purchase vice Shaw, 15 Oct 12.	
John Maclean	2 May 11
Promoted Lieutenant without purchase vice Enright, 10 Dec 12.	

Officers of the Forty Third Light Infantry

Thomas Beckham   7 May 11
Promoted Lieutenant without purchase vice Ridout, 23 Feb 13.

David Fidlor   8 May 11
Died of exhaustion at Madrid, 25 Aug 12.

Nicholas Cundy   9 May 11
Promoted Lieutenant without purchase vice Mayne, 24 Feb 13.

Hon. Chas. Monck   12 Sep 11
Promoted Lieutenant without purchase vice Pollock, 23 Feb 13.

John Neville Robinson   7 Nov 11
Promoted Lieutenant by purchase vice Hobkirk, 18 Mar 13.

Lawrence Steel(e)   21 Nov 11
Formerly Sergeant Major. Adjutant 1st battalion from
    21 Nov 11.
Promoted Lieutenant without purchase, 21 Apr 13.[1]

John Elchin Matthews   16 Apr 12
Promoted Lieutenant without purchase vice Whalley,
    22 Apr 13.

Richard O'Connell   12 May 12
Promoted Lieutenant without purchase vice Capel, 15 Jul 13.

Colin Campbell   13 May 12
Promoted Lieutenant without purchase vice Bevan, 2 Sep 13

Benjamin Hutcheon Edwards   14 May 12
Promoted Lieutenant without purchase vice Folliet, 21 Oct 13.

George Hennell   21 May 12
Promoted Lieutenant without purchase vice J. O'Connell,
    22 Oct 13.

William Carruthers   22 May 12
Promoted Lieutenant without purchase vice E. Freer,
    1 Dec 13.

ENSIGNS JOINING SUBSEQUENTLY
Massey H. Warren   4 Jun 13
Without purchase vice W. Murphy.
Promoted Lieutenant without purchase vice W. Freer, 2 Dec 13.

---

[1] The adjutancy was a subaltern's appointment and the promotion of an adjutant from ensign to lieutenant was made in accordance with his regimental seniority rather than into an existing vacancy.

Appendix 2

Henry Wise Coats   18 Jun 13
    By purchase vice Hood.
    Promoted Lieutenant without purchase vice Brunton, 9 Dec 13.

George Dobson   25 Jun 13
    Without purchase vice Craufurd.
    Promoted Lieutenant without purchase vice Angrove,
        22 Feb 14.

Robert Barham   2 Jul 12
    Without purchase from Lieutenant, East Suffolk Militia.[1]
    Resigned Nov. 12.

John Marshall Miles   10 Dec 12
    Without purchase vice Maclean, from Volunteer 43rd Foot.
    Promoted Lieutenant without purchase vice Baillie.

Richard Fowler   22 Feb 13
    By purchase vice Grubbe.
    Appointed to 95th Rifles, 22 Oct 13.

Edward Rowley Hill   23 Feb 13
    Without purchase vice Beckham, from Volunteer 43rd Foot.
    Promoted Lieutenant without purchase vice B. Murphy.

William Allan   24 Feb 13
    Without purchase vice Cundy.
    Promoted Lieutenant without purchase vice Williams,
        3 Mar 14.

Richard J. Shaw   25 Feb 13
    Without purchase vice Monck.

John Maxwell Williams   22 Apr 13
    Without purchase vice Matthews.

Francis John Greene   15 Jul 13
    Without purchase vice R. O'Connell.
    Appointed as Cornet, 3rd Dragoon Guards, 27 Jan 14.

Alan Browne Baxter   5 Aug 13
    By purchase vice Robinson.

John Finlay   5 Sep 13
    Without purchase vice Campbell.

---

[1] Company officers of the Militia who were able to persuade forty of their men to volunteer as a group to the regular army were entitled to an ensigncy in a regiment of the line and were 'borne, if necessary, as supernumeraries upon the establishment of their battalions, till vacancies occur'.

Officers of the Forty Third Light Infantry

	Regimental Seniority
Thomas Thornley (or Thornelly)	21 Oct 13
Without purchase vice Edwards.	
Chichester Fortescue	11 Nov 13
Without purchase vice Fowler.	
Resigned 7 Apr 14.	
John Pollock	25 Nov 13
Without purchase vice Fidlor.	
Robert Mulcaster Auchmuty	1 Dec 13
Without purchase vice Carruthers.	
Promoted Lieutenant by purchase vice Pattenson, 22 Sep 14.	
Jonah Harris	16 Dec 13
Without purchase as Adjutant 2nd Battalion, from Sergeant Major.	
Henry Hatton	23 Dec 13
Without purchase vice Coates, from R. Military College.	
William Kershaw	25 Dec 13
Without purchase from Lieutenant, Derby Militia.	
Robert William Henry Drury	25 Dec 13
Without purchase from Lieutenant, East Suffolk Militia.	
Thomas Handy Bishop	25 Dec 13
Without purchase from Lieutenant, North Gloucester Militia.	
William Considine	22 Feb 14
Without purchase vice Dobson.	
William Cradock	3 Mar 14
Without purchase vice Greene.	
Richard Ponsonby Webb	20 Apr 14
Without purchase vice Hill.	
Richard John Lambrecht	21 Apr 14
Without purchase vice Miles.	
William Powell	24 Apr 14
Without purchase vice Walton.	
William Sharpe	2 Jun 14
Without purchase from East Suffolk Militia.	

PAYMASTERS

John Richards (1st battalion)	13 Jul 09
Died in Portugal, Jun 12.	

	Regimental Seniority
David Fraser (2nd battalion)	11 Oct 10

| Thomas Tierny vice Richards. | 23 Jul 12 |

QUARTERMASTERS

| James Elliott (2nd battalion) | 23 Nov 04 |
| David Williams (1st battalion) | 29 Nov 10 |

SURGEONS

| James Gilchrist MD (1st battalion) | 15 Dec 04 |
| William Jones MD (2nd battalion) | 9 Mar 09 |

ASSISTANT SURGEONS

William Cumin MD (1st battalion)	7 May 07
Promoted Surgeon 88th Foot, 15 Oct 12.	
Richard O'Connell (2nd battalion)	7 Jul 12
Promoted Surgeon 45th Foot, 16 Mar 13.	
William Thompson (2nd battalion)	21 Jul 08
Resigned 12 Nov 12.	

One appointment vacant since 21 Nov 11.

Archibald Hair MD	12 Nov 12
vice the vacancy from Forfar Militia (1st battalion).	
Henry Edwards	15 Oct 12
vice Cumin.	

Appendix 3

ORGANIZATION OF THE LIGHT DIVISION IN JUNE 1812

General Officer Commanding :
 Maj. Gen. Charles, Baron von Alten.
Principal Staff Officers :
 Assistant Adjutant General. Maj. Charles Rowan, 52nd L.I.
 Assistant Quartermaster General. Maj. the Hon James Stewart, 95th
  Rifles.
Right (or 1st) Brigade. (Lt. Col. Andrew Barnard, 95th Rifles)
 1st battalion, Forty Third Light Infantry.
 2nd battalion, Ninety Fifth Rifles (4 companies).
 3rd battalion, Ninety Fifth Rifles (5 companies).
 3rd Portuguese *Caçadores.*
Left (or 2nd) Brigade. (Maj. Gen. John Ormesby Vandeleur)
 1st battalion, Fifty Second Light Infantry.
 1st battalion, Ninety Fifth Rifles (8 companies).
 1st Portuguese *Caçadores.*

SUBSEQUENT CHANGES

Maj. Gen. James Kempt assumed command of the Right Brigade on
 23 March 1813.
Maj. Gen. John Byne Skerrett assumed command of the Left Brigade from
 July 1813 until he went to England on sick leave in September. The
 brigade was thereafter commanded by Lt. Col. John Colborne, 52nd L.I.
 In November 1812 two more companies of 2/95th joined the Right
 Brigade and it was then moved to Left Brigade in exchange for their first
 battalion.
17th Portuguese Line Regiment (2 battalions) joined the Left Brigade in
 April 1813.

[171]

Note. British battalions at their field establishment had ten companies each commanded by a captain with two lieutenants and one ensign. In practice it was unusual to have more than two officers present with each company. There should have been 100 privates in each company, but, in the field, there were seldom more than 70.

Portuguese battalions had seven companies only.

INDEX

Abrantes, 10

Adour, river, 155

Alba de Tormes, 8, 58

Alcala, 54

Alchangue, Mont, 142n

Allowances, *see* Pay

Alpalhão, 12

Alten, Maj. Gen. Charles von, Baron, 4, 116n, 124, 171

Ammunition, waste, 136

Ampudia, 73, 76

Anderson, Capt., 124

Anglo-Portuguese Army, 9, 10n; at Madrid, 34; Douro, 67–8, 75n; Vitoria, 84, 88n, 89, 90, 91; San Sebastian, 125, 127 and n; France, invasion of, 140; casualties, 155n

Aragon, river, 100

Arcangues, 140, 141, 146n; Marquis d', 143n

Arga, river, 98n

Arganda, 54, 55

Argaum, Battle of, 4

Ariñez, 89n, 90n

Armistice of Pleischwitz, 121n

Arronches, 12

Artillery, 78 and n, 128–9 and n; French, 91–2 and n, 97n; transport, 35

Aylmer, Maj. Gen. Matthew, 5th Baron, 137 and n, 153, 158

Badajoz, 6, 7; camp before, 1, 7; casualties, 13, 14, 16n, 18 and n, 19; fortifications, 12; plunder, 7, 17 and n, 18, 21; storming of, 10, 11–19, 123

Baggage, 59, 80, 87, 100, 101, 115; animals, 83; French, 91n, 92

Baillie, Lieut. M. H., 62n, 143, 144, 145, 146, 166

Basque language, 103–4, 110

Bassussary, 141

Bât money, 33 and n, 64

Bâtmen, 60 and n, 100, 137

Battle, and fear, 19, 102–3, 147; storms before, 128, 136

Bayas, river, 83n

Bayonne, 113n, 122, 130, 140, 147

Behobie, 109n

Beresford, Marshal William Carr, 28n, 127n, 158

Berrioplano, 97n

Bidassoa, river, 99n, 107, 116n, 119, 126, 127, 128 and n, 136n

Blakeney, Robert, 53

Blood, Sgt Thomas, 125n

Blues, the (R.H.G.), 74, 92

Bogue, Mr, 13

Booth, Capt. Henry, 63n, 164

Booth, William, 101n

Brock, Capt. Saumarez, 123, 124, 163

Brunswick Light Infantry, 71n
Bulletins, 67, 131 and n
Bull-fighting, 44–8
Burgos, 35, 52 and n, 56, 66, 68, 73, 76–7, 77–8, 79
Burgoyne, John, 101n

Caçadores, 10n, 30–1, 81, 82, 155,
Cadiz, siege, 35
Cadoux, Capt. Daniel, 128n
Campbell, Lieut. Duncan, 152n, 166
Campbell, Col. James, 11, 22, 158
Campbell, Capt. Robert, 124n
Cantabrian mountains, 105
Carr, Lt. Col. Henry William, 21, 158
Caseda, 99, 100, 101
Castaños, General, 69
Castello Branco, 12
Castrejon, 8, 26 and n, 28 and n
Castrillo, 8, 28n
Casualties, 26, 68; at Badajoz, 13, 14, 16n, 18 and n, 19; Burgos, 35; France, invasion of, 120, 141, 146; French, 82 and n, 85, 96, 140, 155; Light Division, 82 and n, 136n, 141; at Petite Rhune, 142n; in Pyrenees, 117n; retreat to Ciudad Rodrigo, 56, 62 and n; at San Sebastian, 125, 126n; Vera, 136n; Vitoria, 85, 90
Cavalry, 73 and n; at Garçia Hernandez, 31n; at Toro, 71
Cedavim village, 21–2
Censorship, 122n
Champ, Capt. Thomas, 144, 163
Chestnut Troop, Royal Horse Artillery, 97n, 129n
Ciudad Rodrigo, 4, 6, 30, 61, 62, 64, 67, 123; retreat to, 56, 60, 61
Clausel, Gen. Count Bertrand, 34, 158; at Castrillo, 28n; Salamanca, 8–9; Vitoria, 85, 98–9 and n

Col de Velate, 102
Cole, Lt. Gen. Hon. Galbraith Lowry, 80, 158
Colours, Hennell with, 107–8
Commissions: and age, 2; backdating, 148 and n; emergency, 121n; means of obtaining, 2, 132 and n; purchase, 1, 2, 24 and n, 132 and n; retiring from, 121
Connaught Rangers, 4, 90n
Conscripts, French, 147 and n
Cook, Lieut. John, 165; at Bidassoa, 116n; Castrejon, 28n; on drilling, 49n; at Garçia Hernandez, 31n; invasion of France, 152; Ibantelli, 118n; at Toro, 72n; at Vitoria, 92n
Courage, 102–3
Courier, The, 133
Courts-martial, 113
Cox & Co., 148
Craufurd, Maj. Gen. Robert, 4, 62 and n
Crispijana, 91n
Crown Mountain, 137 and n
Curtis, Lieut. Samuel, 156

Dalhousie, Lt. Gen. George Ramsay, 9th Earl, at Vitoria, 88n, 158
Dancing, Spanish, 25
Danger, Hennell's emotions in, 19, 102–3, 147
Donaldson, Joseph, 14n, 25n
Donkeys, mating, 75–6
'Douro' (Wellington), 131 and n, 153, 155
Douro, river, 8, 34, 67, 71, 72; fishing party, 21
Dresden, battle of, 131n
Duffy, Maj. John, 91, 163
'Dutch' troops, desertion, 153–4 and n

Eaton, Lieut. Charles, 124n

Ebro, river, 35, 76, 77, 79, 80, 88n, 118

Echalar, 117n

Edwards, Benjamin Hutcheon, 148, 167

Elvas, 10

Endalazza, 127n

Ensigncy, purchase, 2, 132 and n

Entertainments, 21–2, 25, 44–8, 52, 64–5

Esla, river, 71n

España, Don Carlos de, 50n, 138 and n, 158

Espejo, 79, 82

Esquival, 91n

Exchange, regiments, 150 and n, 156

Fear, and battle, 19, 102–3, 147

Ferey, Gen. Claude François, 32n

Fifth Division, 7; at Badajoz, 12, 16 and n; Salamanca, 30; San Sebastian, 66n, 123, 124, 129 and n; on the march, 73, 80; at Hendaye, 119; Bidassoa, 137 and n; Bayonne, 151

Fifty First Foot, at Toro, 71n

Fifty Second Foot, 81; in Madrid, 58n; at San Sebastian, 126n

Firewood, from houses, 76 and n, 133

First Division, 73, 80; at Salamanca, 30; Vitoria, 88; Bidassoa, 120, 137 and n; San Sebastian, 124n, 129 and n; Bayonne, 151, 153

First (Royal) Regiment, 112n

Fishing party, 21

Fitzgerald, Edward, 101n

Fleas, 101 and n, 110

Flogging, 113

Folliet, Lt. George, 125 and n, 148, 165

Food (*see also* Rations); on the march, 72, 79–80, 93, 107, 111, 122; in Portugal, 21, 22, 43; price of, 23, 38, 41, 63, 75, 79, 80, 122, 131; in Spain, 38, 41, 43, 59, 73, 79

Forage, 123, 131, 147; money, 33 and n, 64

Ford, Richard, 37n

Fort Christobal, 16 and n

Forty Fifth, 90–1

Forty Third (Monmouthshire) Regiment of Foot (Light Infantry), 4–5; casualties, 107n, 117n, 125 and n, 126, 136n; Hennell joins, 23, 25; lieutenants, 156; officers, 162–70; reviewed, 69; Second Battalion, 132n, 148, 156; at Salamanca, 30n; retreat to Ciudad Rodrigo, 62 and n; at Vitoria, 88, 91; in Pyrenees, 107n, 116, 117n; at San Sebastian, 125 and n, 126; at Gallegos, 133n; at Vera, 136n; Nivelle, 142n; in United States, 156

Fourth Division, 5; at Badajoz, 7, 16n; Castrejon, 26n; Salamanca, 30; on the march, 73, 80; at Palencia, 74; Bayas, 83n; at Vitoria, 88 and n, 90, 123; Pamplona, 97–8, 99; in Pyrenees, 116, 117; at San Sebastian, 124n, 126, 129; France, invasion of, 153, 155

Fowke's Regiment, 4

France, allied invasion of, 105, 108–9, 119–20, 140–55; military strategy, 12n, 5–6; Badajoz, 7; Salamanca, 8–9, 67; Burgos, 35, 68; Allied retreat, 56, 57n;

Vitoria, 84–5, 91; Pyrenees, 105–106; Sorauren, 114n; Bidassoa, 119–20; Allied invasion, 140–1

Freer, Edward, 148, 165

French army: destruction of property, 96, 97, 98, 110, 117; invasion of Portugal, 5, 12n, 21; relations with British soldiers, 110, 142–3, 151n, with French people, 143 and n, with Spanish people, 23, 104; retreat from Spain, 95–6, 106

Frontier, Spanish-French, 119–39

Fuentes de Onoro, 4

Fuses, 90n, 112

Gallegos, 64–5, 133 and n

Gallipenza, 99

Garçia Hernandez, 31–2 and n, 58

Garnier, Rosalie, 157

Gazan, Count H. T. M., 159; at Vitoria, 91n; wife, 97n

General Orders, on plunder, 108–9 and n

German units, 31–2, 58, 77 and n, 97

Giron, General, 137n

Gomm, Lt. Col. William, 62n, 130n

Gordon, Col. James Willoughby, 56

Graham, Lt. Gen. Sir Thomas, 159; on the Douro, 68; at Vitoria, 84, 88 and n, 91; Bidassoa, 99n

Grande Rhune, La, 120, 137 and n, 138n

Greenwood and Cox, 150

Guadiana river, 6

Guarda, 12n

Guerrillas, 5, 50–1, 67, 99n, 108

Guns, field, 78 and n, 128–9 and n; transport, 35; French, 91–2 and n, 97n

Hamilton, Lt. William, 124n

Hanger, Col. George, 144n

Harvest, in Spain, 42–3, 73, 79, 80, 133

Harvest, Lt. Augustus, 124n, 125

Haverfield, Capt. William, 30n, 163

Heaphy, Thomas, 131n

Hearn, Lt. Col. Daniel, 89 and n, 146n, 162

Hendaye, 119, 127n

Hennell, George, 1; acting, 22, 64; commission, 1, 2, 23–4, 132 and n, 142n, 148, 167; drawing, 2; escorts prisoners, 49–50; exchange, 150, 156; family background, 1, 2; financial affairs, 2, 27, 32–3, 64, 132 and n; health, 27, 32, 33, 38, 52–3, 62, 77, 134; to 2nd Batt., 132, 148, 150, 156; under fire, 19, 102–3, 144–6; as volunteer, 1–2; wounds, 142n, 148, 156; writing, 2, 27

Hill, Lt. Gen. Sir Rowland, 68, 72, 159; at Badajoz, 7; Tagus, 35, 54 and n; Madrid, retreat, 56; Salamanca, 58, 59; Vitoria, 84, 89n; Maya pass, 112; France, invasion, 140–1, 152, 154–5; Nive, 154–5

Hobkirk, Capt. Samuel, 143, 144, 145, 146, 147, 164

Hope, Lt. Gen. Sir John, 151, 152, 153, 159

Horses, 32–3, 53, 59, 60, 64, 147; injury, 79; mating, 75–6; price, 139

Houlton, Lieut. George, 91, 165

Household Troops, 74, 92, 100, 103

Huebra, river, 61, 69

Hundred Days, 157

Hunt, B/Lt. Col. John, 124 and n

Hussar Brigade, 77; at Toro, 71n, 73; plunder, 103 and n

Ibantelli, *see* Pic d'Ibantelli
Irun, 109n, 129n
Isar, 76, 77

Jaca pass, 129 and n
Joseph, King of Spain, 5, 159; at Madrid, 34, 35, 37, 39n; and Allied retreat, 56; at Valencia, 57n; at Portuguese frontier, 67; at Palencia, 74; Vitoria, 84, 85, 91n, 105; in retreat, 96, 99; at Pamplona, 98n
Jourdan, Marshal J. B., 56, 57, 159; at Vitoria, 89n, 91n

Kempt, Maj. Gen. James, 126, 144, 146n, 155, 159, 171
Kilpatrick, Sgt William, 125
Kincaid, John, 113n
King's German Legion, 77 and n, 82n
Kruse, Col., 153

Ladders, scaling, 7, 14–15 and n, 72 and n
Lanceros de Castilla, 50n
Lang, Ensign James, 13, 14, 18
Lantadilla, 76
Larpent, Judge Advocate, 69n, 131n, 133n, 138n
Law, martial, 17 and n, 131
Lecumberri, 113n
Leipzig, 140, 147n
Le Marchant, Gen. Gaspard, 132n
Leon, Juana Maria de los Dolores de, 17n
Lesaca, 122, 126, 127
Letters from front, publication, 122 and n
Levinge, Sir Richard, 3
Leyza, 116n

Life Guards, 74, 92
Light Division, 4–5; casualties, 82n, 136n, 141; organization, 171–2; in sieges, 66 and n; at Badajoz, 7, 16n; at Castrejon, 26n; Salamanca, 29, 30 and n; Madrid, 58n; retreat, 60; on the march, 73, 84, 116n; Palencia, 74; San Milan, 82n; Vitoria, 88n, 122; and French retreat, 97n; in Pyrenees, 106, 113n, 115, 116n; Bidassoa, 107n; Grande Rhune, 120; San Sebastian, 126; Vera, 136n; France, invasion, 140–1
Lisbon, 119
Logroño, 99n
Longa, Maj. Gen. Francisco, 108, 136, 139, 159
Looting, *see* Plunder
Lyra, HMS, 112n

McArthur, Capt. Archibald, 11, 13, 15
M'Carthy, Lieut. J. E. C., 15n, 18n
Macintosh, James, 133n
Madrid, 34–5, 36–42, 49–50, 52; bull fight, 44–8; La China Fort, 49; citizens, and Allied troops, 38; fashion in, 41–2; funeral, 50; El Escorial, 36–7; officers' quarters, 49; Palacio Real, 39 and n; Pantéon de los Reyes, 37n; poor, 52; prisoners, escorting, 39–40; Real Academia de Bellas Artes, 39–40 and n; Retiro fort, 37n, 49n, 57 and n; retreat from, 56, 57–8
March, Capt. Charles Lennox, Earl of, 25, 117, 159
Marching, 25–6; halting after, 93; in mountains, 10, 100–2, 110, 113, 114; preparations for, 54–5;

in wet weather, 59, 60, 95–6, 107, 111, 113

Marmont, Marshal A. F. L. de, 159; at Salamanca, 8, 22, 23, 59n; Portuguese invasions, 12n; at Castrejon, 26 and n; Garçia Hernandez, 58; wounds, 32 and n, 59n

Maucune, Gen. Anthoine Louis, 81n, 82n

Maya pass, 112, 113n, 115, 130

Medina, de Pomar, 79, 80

Mina y Epoz, Francisco, 99 and n, 159

Monck, Ensign Hon. Charles, 64n

Moniteur, 131n

Monreale, 99, 101

Monteaya, 137n

Moore, Sir John, 4, 62

Morales, 71n, 73n

Morillo, Maj. Gen. Pablo, 90n, 159–60

Mules, 59, 83

Napier, George, 32n, 90n

Napier, Lt. Col. William, 160, 163; at Castrejon, 26n; Salamanca, 30n; Olmedo, 32n; San Sebastian, 124 and n; on 'Vetus', 133 and n; Pasajes, 137n; Arcangues, 146n, 147; peace, 148 and n; Bayonne, 151, 154

Napoleon, and Russia, 5, 35, 67; in Madrid, 38, 39n; and Vitoria, 105, 114n; and Pyrenees, 119; Pleischwitz, 121n; Dresden, 131n, Leipzig, 140, 147; propaganda, 143; conscripts, 147 and n; peace, 148n

New Orleans, 156

Ninety Fourth Foot, 1, 3–4, 10; at Badajoz, 16n

Ninety Fifth Rifles, 80, 81; at Vitoria, 88; at Ariñez, 90n; in Pyrenees, 116; on French frontier, 136, 151, 152

Nive, river, 140, 141, 147, 155

Nivelle, river, 137, 142n

O'Connell, Lieut. John, 123, 124 and n, 125, 132 and n, 142n, 148, 165

Officers: drilling, 49 and n, 52; of Forty Third, 162–70; promotion, 132n, 148 and n

Olite, 99, 100

Olmedo, 32n

Oman, Sir Charles, 1

Orange, Lt. Col. William, Prince of, 64 and n, 160

Ostiz, 102

Oxfordshire and Buckinghamshire Light Infantry, 5

Palencia, 74–5

Palmer, Sgt, 155

Pamplona, siege of, 85, 96, 97 and n, 98 and n, 99, 105, 114 and n, 115 and n, 117, 119, 130; surrender, 98n, 129 and n, 138 and n, 140

Pasajes, 119, 125n, 135, 137 and n

Pay, 33n, 103, 132 and n; half-pay, 121 and n, 147–8, 150, 156–7

Peace, 123, 147, 148 and n

Pensions, 148 and n

Perceval, Lieut. James, 124 and n

Percival, Capt. W., 18n

Pesada, 79

Phillipon, Gen. Baron Armand, 6, 160; at Badajoz, 11, 12, 16 and n

Pic d'Ibantelli, 117n, 118n, 130

Pickets, attack on, 151 and n, 152n

Picton, Lt. Gen. Sir Thomas, 1, 160; character, 24, 25n; health, 24n;

and Hennell, 10–11, 23–4; and Portuguese troops, 10n; at Badajoz, 7, 24n; Vitoria, 88n
Picurina fort, 7
Plays, performed by soldiers, 52, 64–5
Plunder, by British troops, 25n, 54, 81–2, 103, 133–4, at Badajoz, 7, 17 and n, 18; Vitoria, 92 and n, 95; in France, 108–9, 147 and n; at San Sebastian, 130; by Spanish, 138–9, 140, 147n
Portalegre, 10, 12
Portugal: French Army of, 8, 12n, 22, 34, 82n, 85, 114n; French invasions, 5, 12n, 21; relations with British troops, 10; units, 4, 10 and n, 67, 155
Prague conference, 119, 121
Prisoners, exchange, 146
Profanity, officers', 103
Promotion, *see* Commissions
Puebla, La, 84, 89n
Puente Arenas, 79
Puerto de Somport, 129n
Purchase of commissions, 1, 2, 24 and n, 132 and n
Pyrenees, 105–18; beauty of, 102, 112

Quarter, 17n
Quintananiar, 79

Range of fire, 144 and n
Rations, 33n, 53 and n, 58, 118, 154; lack of, 56, 61, 62, 79, 93, 113, 118n
Refugees, 117–18
Regiments, exchange, 150 and n
Reille, Gen. Honoré, 82n, 83n
Religion, 103

Retreat, Allied, to Ciudad Rodrigo, 56, 59
Review of troops, 69 and n
Rhune, La, 140; Grande, 120, 137 and n, 138n; Petite, 142n
Ridout, Lieut. George, 30n, 62, 164
Robinson, Rev. H. B., 16n
Roncesvalles pass, 113n, 114n, 138
Ross, B/Lt Col. Hew Dalrymple, 28n, 97n, 129 and n, 160
Royal Green Jackets, 5
Royal Horse Artillery, 97n, 129n
Royal Military College, 2
Royal Navy, 112 and n, 119
Royal Scots Regiment, 112n
Rueda, 25
Rutherford, Ensign, 146

Ste Barbe redoubt, 138n
St Jean de Luż, 126, 137, 140, 143, 151n
St Pierre d'Irube, 141
Salamanca, 8–9, 22–5, 29, 30 and n, 34, 67, 69; retreat from, 56
Salvatierra, 96
Sanchez, Maj. Gen. Don Julian, 50 and n, 71, 160
San Estevan, 107, 113, 115
Sanguessa, 99, 101
San Marcial, 128n
San Milan, 82n
San Sebastian, siege of, 85, 105, 107n, 109; storming, 112 and n, 113n, 119, 123–6; surrender, 129, 130, 137
Santander, 77, 148
Santarem, 10
Santoña, 85, 129n
Saragossa, 99n
Schaumann, A., 43n
Scots Brigade, 4

Second Division, 72, 73; at Vitoria, 88; France, invasion of, 140

Segovia, 32, 38

Seringapatam, 4

Seventh Division, in retreat, 61; on the march, 73; at Vitoria, 88, 122; Pyrenees, 109, 116, 137; San Sebastian, 125 and n, 127, 129; France, invasion of, 153, 155

Sierra de Aralar, 105, 113n

Simmons, George, 97n

Simpson, Capt. Robert, 144, 164

Sixth Division, at Salamanca, 22 and n, 30; on the march, 73; and Clausel, 99; France, invasion of, 140, 155

Skerrett, Brig. John, 128n, 171

Sleeping, conditions, 57, 58, 59, 60, 61, 75, 101, 110, 111, 129

Smith, Capt. Harry, 17n

Snodgrass, Maj. Kenneth, 125, 126n, 127

Soldiers, before a battle, 102–3, 117; marching, 54–5, 115–16 and n; at rest, 93

Somerset, Lt. Col. Lord Fitzroy, 64–6, 77, 160, 163

Sorauren ridge, 105, 106, 114n

Souham, Gen. Joseph, 59n, 160

Soult, Marshal Nicholas, 160; mistakes, 56; and plunder, 98n; and Wellington, 147; at Cadiz, 34, 35; Aranjuez, 54; and Army of the South, 57n; at Salamanca, 58–9; in Pyrenees, 105, 114n, 115; at San Sebastian, 119, 125n, 126, 127, 129; Pamplona, 131; and Allied invasion, 141, 152, 154–5

Spain: bull-fighting, 44–8; casualties, 50n; dress in, 41–2; food, 38, 41, 43, 59, 73, 79; funerals, 50; guerrillas, 5, 50–1, 67, 99n, 108; harvest, 42–3, 73, 79–80, 133; manufactures, 42; men, 41–42; poor, 52; relations with British troops, 38, 74, 77, 100, 118; religious art, 50; troops, 50 and n, 58, 67, 68, 127 and n, 137, 138 and n; vineyards, 43; women, 42

Sparrow, HMS, 112n

Spies, 143

Statesman, The, 133

Steel, Lt. Lawrence, 145, 167

Stewart, Lt. Gen. Sir Charles, 142 and n, 160

Storming party, volunteers, 123–5

Storms, before battle, 128, 136

Subijana de Morillas, 83n

Suchet, Marshal Louis Gabriel, 35, 57, 99, 129n, 160–1

Sumbilla, 116n

Surtees, William, 18n, 113n

Surveillante, HMS, 112n

Sutton, Maj. Matthew, 148n

Tafalla, 98, 99, 100

Tagus, river, 34–5, 56

Third Division, 5, 10, 66n; at Badajoz, 7, 12, 16; Salamanca, 8, 30; on the march, 73; at Vitoria, 88, 90, 122; and French retreat, 98, 99; France, invasion of, 140, 146, 155

Thirty Ninth (Dorsetshire) Foot, 156

Times, The, 133 and n, 135, 142

Tolosa, 113n

Tomkinson, Capt. William, 28n

Tordesillas, 8, 25, 26n

Tormes, river, 30, 69

Toro, 71–3

Toulouse, 156

Tovar, 76, 79
Tres Puentes, village, 84, 89n
Troops, *see* Soldiers
Tudela, 99

Uniform, 1–2, 25, 33n, 64
Urumea estuary, 126n

Valencia, occupation of, 5; attack on, 57 and n
Valladolid, 32, 34, 38, 73
Vandermaesen, General, 128n
Vera, 107 and n, 109, 111, 116, 122, 126, 135; heights, 136n
'Vetus', 133 and n
Videttes, 142, 151n
Vila Franca, 10
Villaba, 98, 99
Villalta, 79
Villasandino, 76
Villefranque, 155n
Vitoria, 68, 82n, 84–5, 86, 87–93, 122
Volunteers, 1–2; for storming party, 123–5

War, horror of, 14, 18, 19; laws of, 17 and n, 131
War Office, fees, 33n
Wellington, Arthur Wellesley, Duke of: strategies, 4, 5–6, 34–35, 56, 67–8, 83n, 84–5, 105, 119–20, 140–1; Badajoz, 7, 16 and n; Salamanca, 7–8, 30 and n, 34, 58; Castrejon, 26n; Burgos, 35, 78 and n; Madrid, 34–5, 37n, 38 and n; retreat, 56, 67; Toro, 72; Vitoria, 84–5, 90n, 91, 103 and n; Pyrenees, 105–6; Bidassoa, 119–20; France, invasion of, 119–120, 140–1; San Sebastian, 119, 124; Pamplona, 119, 138n; affability, 131–2; bases, 77n, 119; at bull-fight, 44, 45, 46; and censorship, 122n; and Light Division, 4–5, 66 and n, 124; pickets, attacks on, 151n; on plunder, 92n, 103 and n, 109n, 138–9, 147n; and Portuguese troops, 127n; prisoners, exchange, 146n; reviews troops, 69; and Soult, 147, 155; and Spanish troops, 51n; on taking firewood, 76n; and 'Vetus', 133n
West, Mr, 3, 27, 32
Williams, Cornet William, 26n
Wimpffen, Don Luis, 64n
Windham, William, 47 and n
Wolfe, General, 4
Worcester, Lt. Henry Somerset, Marquess of, 25, 161
Wylly, H. C., 25n
Wynyard, Lt. and Capt. M. J., 148n

Yanci, 116n

Zadorra, river, 84
Zalain de Lesaca, 125n